COUNTRYBLAST

COUNTRYBLAST

YOUR COUNTRYSIDE
NEEDS YOU
NOW

CLIVE ASLET

Drawings by
MICHAEL HEATH
with apologies to Thomas Bewick

JOHN MURRAY

Text © Clive Aslet 1991
Illustrations © Michael Heath 1991

First published in 1991
by John Murray (Publishers) Ltd
50 Albemarle Street, London W1X 4BD

British Library Cataloguing in Publication Data
Aslet, Clive 1955–
   Countryblast.
   1. Great Britain. Countryside. Conservation
   I. Title
   333.76160941

   ISBN 0–7195–4945–0

Designed by Mary Staples
Filmset by Wearside Tradespools, Fulwell, Sunderland
Printed in Great Britain by The Bath Press.

To Caroline and James

I would like to thank Jenny Greene, editor of Country Life, *for encouraging me in writing this book. I must also thank Gordon Winter, who read the manuscript, Caroline Knox, who edited it, and my wife Naomi, without whom it could not have been written.*

CONTENTS

INTRODUCTION

Woe unto them that join house to house,
that lay field to field, till there be no
place, that they may be placed alone in
the midst of the earth!
Isaiah 5:8

Over the past ten years the British countryside has changed. That is nothing new: the countryside is always changing as farming practices evolve and trees are planted. But recent changes have little to do with growing things, except for the fact that farmers are not required to produce as much as before. The changes result instead from a host of other uses, which produce nothing. Green fields and pretty villages suffocate beneath an eiderdown of culs-de-sac, filling stations, golf courses, corporate lodges, holiday villages, heritage centres, water parks, leisure pools, pleasure domes, superstores and car parks. Thirty years ago most people who lived in the country had some connection with agriculture. The New Countryman does not relate to the countryside in that way. He probably does not work in it: he is there for recreation.

Partly as a result of these changes, the government now says that the countryside should be protected, not just for the benefit of agriculture but 'for its own sake'. The fact that the countryside gives enjoyment to millions of people is enough to justify such a policy. Unfortunately the rush to exploit this enjoyment commercially, as though it were a new crop, has put at risk some of the very qualities for which the countryside is loved. While changes in farming can generally be reversed, the bricks and concrete which seem to be necessary to enable people to live and relax in wholesome country surroundings will be with us forever.

Yet buildings, including new ones, are essential to the working of the countryside. The countryside is not only a matter of open spaces: for many people, the majority of the time they spend 'in the countryside' is in fact passed in houses, shops, pubs and gardens. 'Walking' is probably done as much along village streets as across hill and dale. Inevitably these man-made surroundings are just as liable to change as green fields. Villages cannot remain completely static: they must be allowed a little leisurely growth, perhaps at the rate of three or four houses every decade. Equally, old farmhouses, cottages and other rural buildings are crucial to our enjoyment of the countryside, and require sensitive handling when they are repaired or adapted, or they will cease to give pleasure. That is why, in writing this book, I have been just as concerned about the appearance of buildings as about the planting of trees.

What some people think of as 'natural' countryside has actually been formed by man's interaction with nature over a period of many centuries. Landscape and buildings have this in common: they both require careful management if the qualities for which we value them are to survive. They both need to be planned.

The first purpose of the book is to analyse the most recent changes in the countryside; the second is to show that effective action can still be taken to influence them. The planning process has come to seem increasingly remote from the individuals whom it affects. During the 1980s successive Secretaries of State for the Environment gathered power unto themselves, subjecting local planning authorities to a reign of terror through their use of the appeals system. Often local authorities feel impotent to act as they feel is right, for fear that their decisions will be overturned and costs awarded against them. This makes it all the more important that individual members of the public – potential voters – make their views known to government. They can do so by directly contacting the relevant Ministries, or by acting through pressure groups; the names and addresses of both are listed in Chapter 22. The chapter 'Rules of Engagement' outlines how the planning system works, and what you can do to influence it.

It is surprising how much can be achieved. Five years ago, when British Telecom announced its intention to replace every one of the fifty-five thousand stately telephone boxes in the country, I wrote a report, with Alan Powers, called *The British Telephone Box ... Take it as Red*. This was published by the Thirties Society, of which I was Honorary Secretary. At that time we had 500 members. British Telecom employs 240,000 people. What was the result of this seemingly unequal contest? British Telecom, being a singularly obtuse and pig-headed organization, is still determined to push through its replacement programme, despite the fact that many of its flimsy new booths already show signs of falling apart. Nevertheless, some thousand telephone boxes have been officially protected through listing. This is a thousand more than would have survived if we had not whipped up a campaign. It represents the largest number of buildings ever to be added to the lists at one time. Telephone boxes are only a detail of the British scene, but what a difference they make to the look of villages and lanes.

Some people may say that, given the enormity of the environmental problems facing the world, preserving the British countryside is a dilettante interest. Far from it. The possible consequences of global warming and ozone depletion make it all the more important that

green fields remain green. If we do not need them for the moment, thanks to the apparent over-production of European agriculture, it is likely that our children or grandchildren may. The contribution which any one individual can make towards safeguarding the future of the planet may seem infinitesimally small. But he or she really can do something useful towards saving the countryside, and that is a start.

1

CRY THE BELOVED COUNTRYSIDE

What kind of countryside do we, the British nation, want? What kind of countryside will we get if we go on treating it as we do? These questions formed the subject of passionate debate in the 1930s, when the South Downs were being choked with motor cars, the town of Peacehaven was spreading like algae over the surface of a beautiful pond, and tentacles of ribbon development had wrapped themselves around the arms, legs and chest of England. We found some of the answers, but over the last decade we have forgotten them.

Once again cars have been allowed to dominate every plan that is made for the countryside. They now determine the shape and placing of all new development, including our wishfully-named new 'towns' and 'villages'. Towns! Villages! The new settlements that bear these names are nothing more than featureless suburbia, without even the saving grace of being near a city. They are all Sub and no Urb. Into our delicate old villages have come swaggering new executive housing estates. Identically dressed dwellings line up around a cul-de-sac like grey-suited managers around a conference table. Double-glazed, double-garaged, double income houses have elbowed their way past church and cottages and eased their bulk on to little infill sites that might once have been a garden or a paddock. Half of a village may have taken more than five centuries to evolve, but the other half will have sprung out, like a pop-up book, in less time than it takes to read a Department of the Environment Planning Policy Guidance note.

The New Countryman is on the move. He hurtles down the motor-

The longest dry-ski slope in the world is now being built by Ski Village Holdings on Teesside. The complete project will include nine slopes as well as Alpine chalets.

way, past the cobalt blue walls of the do-it-yourself store and the toytown roofs of the supermarket, a mere eye-blink from death beneath the fender of a juggernaut. Why is he doing it? He is on the way to the new golf club. You should see it – thirty-six holes, a clubhouse like the QE2, and they are building a new wing so that it can double as a conference centre. Or he may divert to the dry-ski slope or to the marina, more crowded with masts than Cadiz when the Armada assembled. Lovely view of the estuary, so wild-looking. Pity that fifteen thousand oystercatchers have been displaced and that the riverview flats they occupy destroyed the last vestige of true wilderness. Or he may simply head for the hills, and watch helicopters drop soil on mountaintops eroded by the sheer number of visitors. After all, he does have a luxurious timeshare to stay in. Pop on the sunglasses, slip into the iridescent two-tone jogging suit. No need to worry about lowering English skies when he can sip a gin and tonic beneath the palm trees of the El Tropicana club room.

Oh Leisure, he worships you, in leisure centre and in health club. A goat-hoofed god who dances through the countryside, luring three-quarters of the population thither by his Pan-pipes. A bronzed god from Mediterranean shores, or perhaps Miami. No wonder the New Countryman visits his countryside dressed in the baseball cap of another clime.

'The housing element of marinas is seen as particularly important and desirable. The specialist agency Waterside Properties predict that there will be more than 20,000 newly built homes in marinas by 1995.' Investment in Tourism, January–June 1990.

What is left of the old mysteries? Look up into the night sky and, as you search for Orion's belt, a television satellite goes tumbling by. Equally, hope to come upon some special, undiscovered place and there will be a dozen tourist roadsigns pointing to it. Stripped of all their creepers, ancient ruins stand before us cold and naked, mocked by the English Heritage banners flapping round their brows. Wayside telephones find themselves encased in perspex booths, exhaling the stale breath of Manhattan into the rich country air. Verges are trimmed to look like Astroturf. Hedgerows are torn up to make way for parking areas equipped with picnic tables. Our roads have undergone a sort of pedicure at the hands of the highways departments. Roundabouts, curbstones, pavements, rumblestrips, raspberry-coloured tarmac — these things are the painted toenails of the countryside.

According to a survey published by the Countryside Commission, 72 per cent of people questioned prefer to spend their leisure time in the countryside. Only 17 per cent preferred towns and cities.

Extraordinary, this degradation. For the countryside is at the centre of our spiritual life and values. Look at the lengths to which people go to keep a garden or an allotment. The loss of trees, through Dutch Elm Disease or the Great Storm of 1987, struck us with the force of a family bereavement. And over two million people belong to the National

Trust. This is more than belong to all the political parties put together, more than the number of people who go to church on Sundays. Small in scale, quickly changing between one region and another, vulnerable, the British countryside has provoked the protective instincts of generations of campaigners since the eighteenth century. It has fared better than that of Italy or Switzerland, littered with villas, or Ireland, crazed with bungalows. Vast as it is, the United States has little countryside in the sense in which we use the term: its farmed landscapes are not visited for pleasure. The countryside used to be something we did well in Britain. One could hardly say the same for our towns and cities, which, particularly in their recent development, hardly bear comparison with those of Continental Europe.

What do towns and cities have to do with the theme of this book? Everything. The problem of our cities is one and the same as the problem of our countryside. The greatest hope for the countryside is that our towns and cities should become beautiful again.

2

IS YOUR JOURNEY REALLY NECESSARY?

Nineteen eighty-nine was a bad year for the six hundred inhabitants of Tetsworth in Oxfordshire. First they had to fight off the proposal to build the new town of Stone Bassett on their doorstep. They succeeded. It cost them £160,000. But the very day after the Secretary of State for the Environment announced his decision to turn Stone Bassett down, South Oxfordshire District Council received a letter from the Department of Transport. It was a planning application to deposit, on the edge of Tetsworth, a motorway service area of gigantic proportions – the largest ever built in Britain. If approved, the Tetsworth service area will cover 103 acres: the size of a small farm. The site is bigger than Wembley Stadium and three times the size of the village. Once again the residents have had to go into combat, fight a public inquiry (the result of which is awaited) and begin the arduous task of raising from a small community what might be a six-figure sum.

This service area is a glimpse into what our future will be like if we go on allowing ourselves to be dominated by the motor car. It is planned to meet the predicted traffic volumes of 2020. The Department of Transport estimates that, on an average day, the volume of traffic going along this stretch of the M40 will nearly double, from 65,200 vehicles in 1993 to 120,300 in 2020, so parking space for 1,230 vehicles has to be envisaged. In order to conceal this monster in a landscape which offers no natural features to shield it, the Department of Transport – newly sensitive to the environment – will have to erect earthbanks on the scale of a Bronze Age hill-fort. Tetsworth will become the late-twentieth century's Maiden Castle.

Tetsworth is planned as one of the first of a new generation of service stations – seventeen were announced by Paul Channon in 1987. Will they all be Tetsworths? And what are the implications for our forty-one existing service areas, minnows beside the Tetsworth whale? Watford Gap covers eleven acres. Most of the rest occupy between twenty and thirty acres. The largest by a long way, Killington Lake on the M6, is fifty-four acres. Will the time come when they all must be doubled, tripled, quintupled in size? In 1990 Cecil Parkinson tossed £6 billion into the labyrinth of our road system, but even this was not enough to satisfy the road lobby monster that lurks within. Active consideration is being given to the building of even more new roads, funded privately and paid for by tolls. Perhaps the people who support toll roads have been impressed by the American experience, and look forward joyously to the day when most of England has been turned into a New Jersey of highways, thruways, freeways and parkways, with nothing but suburbs in between.

The Department of Transport predicts an eventual doubling of car ownership and, by 2025, an increase of up to 142 per cent more road traffic over 1988 levels. Since some motorways, even in the calm middle of the day, are already apt to grind to a standstill, human understanding can hardly comprehend the enormity of the sums of money – or the miles of fresh tarmac – that would be necessary to have the whole system moving freely in the twenty-first century. Merely building a few new roads or improving old ones will not be enough. Crowded roads put people off travelling: build a new road, however, and they take to their cars – until the new road too is congested. This has been spectacularly demonstrated by the case of the M25.

Fortunately, no government will ever have the money or the will to build enough roads to satisfy fully the demands of car owners and haulage companies. However, this does not mean that the roads which are built will not be sufficient to destroy the countryside. Recall the M3 extension around Winchester and through Twyford Down. Contemplate with horror the proposal to build an East Coast motorway through the North York Moors National Park.

The railways represent one of the great miracles of our age. They have become dirty, uncomfortable, less than wholly reliable, and the most expensive in the world. Yet – and this is the miraculous bit – they are nearly always full. How many more trains would it be physically

English Heritage has calculated that the new roads detailed in the D.o.T.'s 1990 policy document Roads to Prosperity *could destroy or disturb nearly eight hundred and fifty archaeological sites. The cost of rescue archaeology at these sites is estimated at £73 million.*

possible to schedule? And would not these, like new roads, instantly fill up as suppressed demand was released? The railways' present base is so small that, according to the Department of Transport, even a 50 per cent increase in rail traffic would only reduce road traffic by 5 per cent. Now, this in itself would be worth achieving. Most of the car journeys that people make are local. Those over twenty-five miles account for a mere 3.5 per cent of the total number of all journeys travelled. If we could get the long-haul freight traffic on to rail, this would have a major effect on our motorways. Nevertheless, the railways by themselves will not solve our problems.

There are two things we must do. First, we must establish a development policy which makes public transport feasible. Our present approach is to live by the car and die by the car. The motorways and trunk roads have become to us what the rivers and canals used to be before the age of the railways. They are regarded as the principal arteries of communication, around which all new development is based. Superstores, housing estates and business parks batten on to them like leeches. Motorways which once ran with a certain elegance through open countryside are now hedged in on either side by the new version of ribbon development. Naturally, these new developments can only be serviced by road.

Worse, we disperse ourselves around the countryside in such a way that not even buses can cope. Public transport works best when it runs between one area of concentrated population and another. We must learn to live in greater densities. The planners have become frightened of densities of over 100 people per acre because they associate high density with the disaster of high-rise council flats. Fortunately, tower blocks are not the only means of achieving high densities. Terraces of four or five storeys, containing flats and maisonettes, can comfortably achieve densities of up to 160 people per acre. Built around gardens, they can be exceptionally attractive. No new development should be permitted which is not within walking distance of a railway station. This is already appreciated in Sweden – but then, the Swedes do not have the British horror of planning for the future well-being of their society.

Second, we must accept the fact that the great days of uninhibited travel are over. We have come to pitch our expectations of mobility too high. Everyone – or at least everyone who cannot afford a helicopter – will have to think of living on a more local scale. This is not a pious hope, but an inevitable consequence of the increasing congestion of the roads. Even government ministers privately admit that there are no plans to *solve* the traffic problem: it is merely assumed that when congestion on one route becomes unbearable, drivers will find another. When all the available routes become hopelessly clogged, drivers will think hard before setting out. Soon we will find ourselves resurrecting the wartime slogan: Is Your Journey Really Necessary?

Perhaps more and more of us will develop a village ethos, making only short trips between home and work. In theory, computers and the fax machine could mean that many more people work from home. There is little sign of it at present. The death of the office has been widely predicted but, in the mid 1980s, London experienced an office-building boom of unprecedented proportions. Strange though it may seem, we like our offices. We go in for the gossip and the companionship, and it is feared that no one gains promotion by working at home. But undoubtedly the agony of travel will force all but the toughest commuters to live closer to their place of work. Already, unfettered travel – represented by helicopter and private jet – is seen as one of the great luxuries of the late twentieth century.

What does this mean? If we cannot travel so freely, if we must live within easy reach of public transport, in greater densities than before, where will we go? Where will our new development go? The answer can only be, our existing suburbs. They already possess highly developed systems of public transport, and in many cases would benefit from a higher density of development, which would bring with it a greater sense of cohesion and more public buildings. The suburbs could

themselves acquire the facilities of small towns – of inestimable benefit to teenagers who are bored witless with nothing to do. It is possible to imagine more people enjoying what will soon become the ultimate luxury of being able to walk to work.

The alternative – for most of England to become a suburb – is not only unacceptable, it just will not work.

3

SHOPS THE SIZE OF FARMS: THE SUPERSTORE

The latest trend which is helping to ensure Britain develops a terminal state of car-dependency is the superstore or retail park. These monstrous, swaggering supermarkets have, within the space of a decade, barged their way on to the fields surrounding many of our major towns. Like other bullies, superstores do not like to stand on their own: they have recently started to cluster together into so-called retail parks, which are likely to have a supermarket, DIY store, furniture warehouse and seller of 'white goods' (electricals). Tesco and Marks & Spencer, for example, have an arrangement for the joint purchase of out-of-town sites.

In the early days, superstores tended only to occupy sites on marginal land. They have gained confidence since then, and the sites that are now being developed are much more expensive. This not only puts prime farmland at risk but, particularly in the North, blocks the arrival of new industry. Councils anxious to lure incoming firms increasingly find that the best sites – needless to say, those most accessible to the motorway – have been bought for superstores first.

The British public has been taken by surprise. It was quite unprepared for the scale and the pace of the superstore onslaught. No less than 40 per cent of Sainsbury's trading area has been rushed up since 1985; the new build totals nearly 5¼ million square feet. The Argyll Group's annual report boasts of the rapidity with which their new Safeway superstores are erected: even the largest take little more than 50 weeks. Plans for new superstores are rarely called in for a personal decision by the Secretary of State for the Environment. Needless to say, we have no national or regional policies to determine where the new superstores should be placed, or whether they are desirable at all. Indeed, the blitzkreig has been so sudden that little public discussion of any kind has taken place.

There is, however, evidence of mounting irritation at the super-stores' toy town architecture of gables, weathervanes, clocktowers and vast, barn-like roofs – designed to give the illusion that these monstrous buildings are really ever so small and friendly. The architectural detail is applied in the thinnest of veneers, hardly disguising the fact that a superstore is really nothing more than a spreading, industrially-produced warehouse. What is truly appalling, though, is the sheer scale of the things: the amount of land they take up. The new Sainsbury's Savacentre at London Colney in Hertfordshire – the largest British hypermarket to date – covers no less than twenty-three acres. Sainsbury make much of their commitment to 'good quality architecture', reflected in the bright lights and shiny columns of the Savacentre. But most of the site is not architecture at all. It is tarmac. Tarmac for car-parking bays (1800 of them) and tarmac for the lanes along which the cars circulate. Inside, the trolley takes over from the car. Most superstores are not more than one storey tall, thus ensuring the maximum extravagance of space. Who says that there is a shortage of land for homes? These sites could have been developed to provide housing for thousands of people.

Superstores attract customers from within a radius of a dozen miles or more. Not everyone will visit them, but they take enough of the area's shoppers to make the existence of smaller local shops, particularly those in villages, ever more perilous. Planning permission is being sought for more superstores all over the country. But where is the need for a twelve-and-a-half-acre Tesco, for example, outside Cirencester, which is already well served by every variety of small shop? The superstore can only succeed by sucking the life out of local commerce.

Does this matter? Far too much sentimental rubbish is talked about the village shop. Many village shops offer such a dreary service to the customer that they deserve little sympathy when they go out of business. Village shopkeepers must realize that, these days, even rural shoppers are likely to require more than some wizened apples and a jar of Nescafé. However, there will always be some people who, because they have no transport, rely on the village shop for their daily needs.

Less discussed is the case of the small shop in the town. Shopping is one of the few activities that brings a town centre alive during the day – or indeed at any time. If more small shops in towns are turned into offices or building societies, even more people will desert the towns for the suburbs and dispersed settlements which have had such a fatal influence on the countryside. The superstore and the mall have been designed to meet the needs of the baby-boom generation, now entering its thirties and forties. One-stop shopping is an undoubted convenience for these busy young people, often bringing up families. When these same people are in their fifties and sixties, with the children away and much more time on their hands, will their priorities be the same? It is at least arguable that they will prefer shopping in a less stereotyped environment, where they can enjoy personal service and a specialist range of shops. They will find this in the town centre.

People enjoy the variety they find in towns. They particularly seem to like *escaping* the car. Recent studies by the German Institute for Urban Planning and the London-based transport consultancy, TEST, conclude that pedestrianizing towns actually helps trade. This flies in the face of conventional shopkeepers' wisdom, but can easily be demonstrated by a glance at Cambridge or York. Draconian traffic

policies have contributed enormously to the quality of life these towns are seen to offer, and this in turn has persuaded many companies that they wish to be based there. In other words, commercial success here has depended partly on the possibility of making journeys by foot – precisely the transport mode that present government policies do their best to discourage.

Not all towns have been allowed to retain their historic character into the late twentieth century. Too many were disfigured by concrete shopping centres in the 1960s and 70s. These require urgent attention. The big supermarket chains, builders of superstores, continue to make record profits, even in this time of recession. What is needed is a tax on all new construction of superstores, the proceeds of which would go to enhance the historic town centres which they are depriving of trade. By this means, town centres will survive into the age – already dawning in the United States – when the fashion for superstores and shopping malls has passed.

4

THE COUNTRYSIDE
AS PLAYGROUND

Remember the brash, 22-year-old commodity broker, in striped shirt and Wall Street braces, portable phone pressed to one ear, driving a Porsche, earning a fortune and working a sixteen-hour day? Poor yuppie, his mayfly summer has already passed, but he was one of the stock characters of the 1980s. Life for him hardly existed off the dealing floor. He represented the Go-For-It, Cold-Shower, Can-Do economy that came in after Big Bang. There was another side to this coin, however. Just when the yuppie started to emerge from his chrysalis, other groups of people were beginning to find that they were having to work not more, but less. They had an increasing amount of time on their hands. Some of them could be seen ambling off towards Budleigh Salterton, a caravan hitched to the back of the family saloon, relaxed and unhurried, having plucked the fruits of prosperity and retired early to digest them. On average, a retired man has ninety-two hours of free time a week.

Not surprisingly, the retired and the unemployed possess more free time than any other section of the population. But even working people have twice as much holiday, and a considerably shorter working week, than thirty years ago. Yawning gulfs of free time and nothing to do with it! In order to prevent this horror, the government invented 'leisure'.

The terrifying thing about leisure is how many people now want to spend it in the countryside. Three-quarters of us! Hardly anyone seems to have commented on the astonishing revolution in our habits that this represents. The revolution would not have been possible without the motor car. Before the Second World War most people preferred the seaside: at least, that is where they went, because that is where the excursion trains took them. They travelled *en masse*, and there was much to be said for it. Now the British seaside is devoid of glamour. Hoteliers have specialized in offering a uniquely dismal experience to the rump of the holiday market – that part which cannot stir itself to go overseas. Thanks to the car, visits to the countryside are twice as popular. With the car the New Countryman can get practically anywhere, and he does not have to stay there very long before dashing on to the next place.

There was a leisure class before, made up of people who did not need to go out to work, and whose whole education taught them how to pass their time agreeably. But the new leisure class does not have the benefit of this training. They come upon leisure unprepared. Consequently, it is assumed that they have turned into babies again. They find themselves being spoon-fed. Garment manufacturers shrewdly express this infantilism in their clothes. It is epitomized by the jogging suit, a kind of stretchy baby-grow for adults, completely shapeless, devastatingly unflattering for large-bottomed women, with an elasticated waistband to allow the male wearer to eat as much as he wants: the trousers expand with the stomach. Such clothes are the ideal wear for the theme park, where visitors regress to babyhood, because the essence of the theme park is that everything is done for you. You do not have to worry; you do not have to think.

Theme parks grew out of the safari parks of the 1960s. Visitors to the latter drove through with the car windows firmly wound up: those who did not were liable to be eaten by lions. Naturally this tended to keep participation to a minimum. Theme parks have gone somewhat further. They offer a completely passive experience, akin to watching television. Period characters – jolly jack tars in earrings, Mr Micawbers in stovepipe hats – come up to you unbidden. The only difference is that you are not at home, but walking about in the country. Alton Towers, visited by 2.5 million people a year, comes second only to Madame Tussaud's as the most popular tourist attraction currently charging admission.

Themed hotels will be the next development, according to the English Tourist Board. 'In this regard consider plugging hotels onto museums/theme parks', advises that ineffable prose stylist *Investment in Tourism, January–June 1990*. Museums? But of course. With the

appearance of the Jorvik Centre in York, Wigan Pier, and the Tales of Robin Hood, history has become just another 'heritage attraction'. As *Investment in Tourism* continues: 'For the first time culture/history and pure entertainment were brought together under one product'. Pleasure domes, packed with new technology, are likely to cause a 'further blurring at the edges of the themeparks/heritage and museum businesses'.

One, under licence from the BBC, is being planned by the American leisure company D'Artagnan. Previously responsible for converting the Queen Mary in California, they are proposing to build not just a synthetic English village, but a synthetic Ambridge – fictional home of 'The Archers' radio serial – beneath an all-weather plastic bubble in Milton Keynes. This must be the ultimate repackaging of the rural myth, for people who do not want to take the trouble to go there.

Unfortunately it is no longer necessary to visit a theme park or pleasure dome to be in one. Complete villages, particularly in the Cotswolds, have turned themselves into babyfood, offering spoonfuls of 'A Peep at the Past – Village Life at the Old Mill', or the inevitable rural craft museum. This pappy, morris-dancing image of the English countryside, boiled down from James Herriot and Miss Marple television programmes, is purveyed by shops selling woollens, bygones, perfumed soap and souvenirs. Marina developments (there is one proposed for virtually every creek and inlet on the south Devon coast) specialize in this pap. Take Brighton Village Marina. Huddled beneath the cliff and separated from the sea by swathes of car park, the clownish terraces parody the town itself. To reinforce the point, the Beefeater steak house sports onion domes, coloured lime green, that look like a five-year-old's drawing of the Pavilion.

We head for the open spaces and find ourselves in a country park, full of interpretation boards and trail signs. We seek out that desolate and haunted Scottish glen – Glencoe – and still we are not alone. An award-winning air raid shelter, or something which looks very much like one, has been built by the National Trust for Scotland to interpret the famous massacre; the drawings look for all the world as though they come from the back of a cornflakes packet. What a stimulus to the imagination! South of the border, of course, we are rarely allowed to visit any ancient building in the nation's keeping without passing through the purgatory of a hideously jarring visitor centre. Come on the wrong day, and theme park Britain will be out in full force. English Heritage, not confident enough to allow great buildings to cast their spell in quietude, stages mock battles (Roundheads in Pierre Cardin specatacles) in a doomed effort to bring the past alive. They do for the English Civil War what *Carry on Cleo* did for the Roman Empire.

The English Heritage logo, that painfully dated emblem of corporate design, has become a danger signal. To see it flapping on a flagpole, in place, perhaps, of the cross of St George or the family banner, warns that the monument we approach will have been denuded of all romance. Forget the crumbling battlements; what we have here is, in tourist parlance, a 'wet-weather facility'. We are aware of the message long before the ruin itself hoves in view. In their use of signs English Heritage are capable of a positive genius for the wrong response. Longtown is a tiny Herefordshire village in the Welsh Marches. Like nearly every other settlement round about, it has a castle. No one is likely to miss it. But lest one might have the pleasure of coming upon it unprepared, English Heritage has gone to the expense of erecting no fewer than four brown signs around the village showing the way to it. The site is too small to merit an attendant in a hut, so there is no commercial benefit; the signs just clutter up the countryside in a misplaced exercise in public relations.

The nation's playground: that is indeed what the countryside has become. But must the playground be that of a kindergarten?

Government has failed to look critically at leisure. Because of the fear that a population with time on its hands will become restive, it has tended to see the provision of leisure facilities, in any form, as unreservedly a good thing. For example, the Sports Council, a government agency, supports the building of leisure centres which, even at Kendal in the Lake District, are no more than ugly industrial sheds.

Leisure is now so big that careful thought must be given to its effect on the countryside. Take the question of new golf courses. There is intense resistance to new golf courses in Japan and the United States, partly because of the level of chemicals necessary to keep the greens verdant. But in Britain they are regarded benignly by the D.o.E., and as a result local authorities find it extremely hard to turn them down. In a controversial report, the Royal and Ancient in St Andrews has declared that Britain needs no fewer than seven hundred new courses by the end of the century to fulfil the predicted demand. So fast have the planning applications come in that some counties will achieve their quota within five years.

Of course, some new golf courses are needed. But, as with any leisure

Leisure buildings tend not to come by themselves. Developers know that they can be of enormous benefit in giving retail and housing developments an identity. Recent proposals include the £100 million Norwich Riverside (to include a hundred-bed hotel, swimming pool, ten-pin bowling alley, housing and shops) and Plymouth City Council's schemes for eleven miles of waterfront, for which an investment of over £1 billion will be required. There are also plans to make Plymouth the site of a 700 foot tower, the centrepiece of a new leisure and retail development.

application, the siting must be right. A beautifully-designed golf course can have some of the qualities of a fine landscape park. In the urban fringes – those difficult areas of not-quite-countryside on the edges of towns – golf courses can be an enhancement, providing well-maintained open spaces in areas which, because of vandalism and trespass, may be difficult to farm. But they rarely look well in open countryside, because they are too obviously artificial and are designed to the wrong scale. The worst examples operate a scorched-earth policy, removing all existing trees before instigating new planting. It will take scores of years before the new trees mature and look comfortable with their surroundings. Too often the very landscape of the golf course represents a suburban intrusion. In part this derives from the need to squeeze eighteen holes on to a site that may be 120 acres or less; more generous sites give room for more trees to be planted and existing features in the landscape to be retained. Nevertheless, the local authority has little control over planting when an application is granted.

New golf courses are not on the whole created by groups of enthusiasts for their own use, but by businessmen who intend to make money. Generally their profit does not come from the course itself, but from the club house and other buildings that go with it. Often the club house has a mysterious habit of metamorphosing itself into a conference centre. Many golf course proposals are accompanied by housing schemes. Do we need the golf courses so much that we are prepared to accept the houses that go with them?

Any new use of the countryside must be reversible. We have an apparent surplus of farmland at the moment, but we do not know when we will need it again. Golf courses can be ploughed up, and that is much in their favour; but it is unlikely that the land occupied by their associated buildings will ever return to grass. Leisure activities are acutely sensitive to fashion. They must be allowed only the minimum of permanent structures to house them, or one day they will become the equivalent of 1930s cinemas, hundreds of which are now redundant and decaying.

One of the difficulties of leisure is not just that we have so much more of it, but that we can afford to do things on such a big scale. What might be called the hardware of recreation – from powerboats to hot-air balloons – has become increasingly costly and elaborate. Booker airfield, on the edge of High Wycombe, is busier than Manchester International Airport. Camper vans have grown bigger than

Britain's imports of food and live animals, excluding drink, amounted to £9 billion in 1989. We only exported £5 billion.

armoured personnel carriers. Inevitably this will lead to friction between the different groups of new countryside users. There are already signs of it. Ramblers have long battled with the grouse shooters who seek to keep them off the moors. Of more recent date is the ire of the fisherman who finds the calm of the riverbank shattered by a flotilla of white-water canoeists. Fell walkers, enjoying the peace of the mountainside, do not relish the whine of the trail bike. The gardener shakes his fist at the droning microlight. Horse riders may be less than sympathetic to the rampaging of war-games enthusiasts firing ink balls.

Conflict will be reduced if a larger area of land is made available for public use. The decline in profits from agriculture has caused farmers to look harder at how they use their principal asset. Recently the idea of Environmental Land Management Services has been evolved. These will enable farmers to enter into agreements with particular groups – perhaps a fishing club, perhaps the local authority – to manage their farms for the group's benefit. The farmer does not lose ownership or control of his land; he merely provides a service for the group. For example, birdwatchers might pay the farmer to ensure that conditions on his farm are right for visiting redshank. In East Anglia, a group of horseriders have already made ELMS-type agreements with no fewer than sixty local farmers to create and maintain eighty miles of new bridleways. This is an imaginative development which will benefit both farmers and public. You might think of pressing your local council, both county and district, to find out what they have done to encourage such partnerships in the countryside.

There is no reason why this new leisure access should degenerate into the mashed banana described earlier in the chapter. Surely the public itself does not want it. What is so sad is that some of the worst of the baby-food is dished out by government agencies and local authorities.

5

DEATH BY TOURISM

When leisure gets completely out of hand, causing people to rush around the countryside in order to spend their free time somewhere else, it is called Tourism. No one will be surprised to discover that this is a gigantic industry, with a worldwide turnover of $450 billion. It accounts for 5 per cent of all trade throughout the world. The number of foreigners visiting Britain currently stands at 17.2 million a year, and it seems to be on the way up. Before the Gulf crisis the British Tourist Authority was predicting that numbers would reach 28 million by the year 2000. Also growing is the time that some Britons are able to spend travelling in their own country. One in four of the holiday-going class (60 per cent of the population) now takes a second holiday, as opposed to one in six in 1971. This second holiday is likely to be in Britain. Including short breaks, the British take no fewer than 73 million holidays in Britain every year.

Tourists used to be interested principally in visiting the big cities and the seaside resorts. Now their destinations are more diffuse. The volume of literature on the countryside is infinitely greater than, say, before the Second World War. Consequently, the tastes of more intrepid tourists have become more demanding. There are more people who want to go to wilder, remoter locations. The solitary walker is liable to find his path usurped by a crocodile of brightly-coloured anoraks. In their wake come other visitors, lured by a mirage of natural beauty but uncertain quite what it is or how to possess it. The countryside is in fashion. Recognizing this, developers have rushed to

package the experience so that customers can enjoy all the things associated with the countryside (and some which are not) without having to tire themselves out by going on a muddy walk. They may not even have the sensation of being in the British countryside at all.

About a decade ago, some local authorities realized that their municipal swimming pools lacked pzazz. For many people swimming had come to be associated with package-holidays abroad, and the new 'Leisure Pools' which now appeared in a flash of blue glass sought to recapture the escapism of those fortnights in the sun. Outside it is Barnsley in the sleet. Inside, around the café tables, the bathers luxuriate in a piñacolada paradise of tropical vegetation, waterfalls and 'flumes' (corkscrew tunnels down which children shoot on a rush of water). It might be Menorca in July. This became the style, too, of the time-share developments which have been plaguing our National Parks. Some dozen were constructed in the Lake District before the Department of the Environment decided, belatedly, that enough was enough. 'Rare species of palm tree from Mexico and colourful tropical birds thrive in the controlled climate', coos one promoter's brochure. Wonderful it must be to see the weatherbeaten hill farmers, given free entry in an attempt to curry local favour, sipping drinks around the pool.

Some forty applications to build major tourist complexes in our National Parks are still current.

The latest idea, unknown in Britain before 1986, is to create what are euphemistically known as holiday villages; these, rather in the manner of the old-fashioned Butlin's holiday camps of the 1950s, offer a complete range of holidays within the confines of the development. But the world has moved on since Butlin's: these are very sophisticated and elaborate projects indeed. A taste is given by Glyn Rhonwy, a proposal for a lakeside site just outside the Snowdonia National Park. 'View to Snowdon' is one of the attractions marked on the developers' map. Others include cable car, ski centre, hotel, restaurant, Leisure Pool, three hundred houses, clay-pigeon shoot, boat moorings and Quarry Auditorium, in which an old slate quarry would be glassed over and turned into a 'mafan drofannol' (which is Welsh for tropical paradise). Glyn Rhonwy has not been given planning permission. Center Parcs however, (originally a Dutch firm, now controlled Scottish and Newcastle Breweries) has already built holiday villages at Sherwood and Thetford. It wants to build another one, covering 400 acres, at Bovey Tracey in Devon. This will include 700 villas and a huge glass dome covering the swimming pool, waterways and six 'eating outlets'. Within the glass dome visitors will be sealed off from the surrounding environment, though it is less certain that the latter will be sealed off from the dome.

The tourist problem is not simply one of numbers. Despite the recent increase in second holidays, the total of nights which British people spend holidaying in Britain is actually smaller than twenty years ago. What has increased enormously is the amount of money changing hands. Ever more elaborate facilities are constructed to persuade visitors to part with their cash. Meanwhile the raw material upon which the industry relies – things to see – is literally being worn away. Seaside towns became crowded during the season, but did not suffer physically from the effects of over-visiting. This is not the case with the more fragile attractions in the countryside, to which fashion is directing more and more people. The demand is concentrated and continuous. Once there was an off-season, but now hoteliers in the most visited parts of the countryside say that their rooms are full year round.

Country house visiting has now reached epidemic proportions. The National Trust has not entirely shed the attitudes evolved when it was a cosy group of like-minded dilettanti, rather than what it has become: the largest landowner in Britain after the Crown. Beatrix Potter's little farmhouse, Hill Top, in the Lake District, is opened to the public just as it might have been forty years ago. But visitors no longer comprise just a handful of Peter Rabbit enthusiasts on a wet afternoon. Eighty thousand people squeeze through it every year. They come – they *keep* coming – despite the fact that it is not advertised or marked by a road sign, and that there is not really very much to see. Yet the National Trust does not take effective measures to limit admissions.

Snowshill in Worcestershire is an even greater problem, because the house contains – or did – many collections formed by the architect Charles Paget Wade. Wade's taste was hardly conventional: he had an obsessive love of intricate objects and theatrical effects. Until recently it embarrassed the Arbiters of Taste within the Trust. Now it happens to resemble the favourite style of glossy decorating magazines. But the more people who shuffle through the house – 'bum to belly', as the administrator graphically puts it – the less true to Wade's vision it becomes. Tables crowded with little objects have had to be cleared; a regrettable second staircase has been inserted to facilitate the flow of bodies. Visitors swarm ant-like over the little village in which the house is located. Why cannot access be controlled? Many historic houses in the United States operate on a limited ticket system, for which booking in advance is necessary. It is difficult to avoid the suspicion that visitor figures, rather than quality of visitor experience, have been taken as the yardstick of success.

Snowshill is an exception. At other properties, such as the recently opened Calke Abbey, the Trust has taken greater trouble to manage visitor numbers. Nevertheless, one must question whether the sheer volume of bums and bellies passing through some houses – 200,000 a year in the case of Polesden Lacey in Surrey, for example – is not posing a long-term risk to the delicate fabric of the building. These structures were, after all, built as family houses, for the occupation of, at most, a few dozen people. The Trust's work in maintaining the surroundings of its houses, while still finding room for the necessary lavatories and teashop, is often of a very high standard. But the character of any place will change if the intensity of visiting is pushed beyond a certain point. Gravel paths will replace grass ones, uneven farmyards will be levelled and steps will give way to ramps. Gardens, such as Sissinghurst Castle and Hidcote Manor, are particularly vulnerable. In a recent issue of the gardening journal *Hortus* (Autumn 1990), Dawn MacLeod, who lived at Inverewe on the west coast of Scotland during the last years of its existence as a private house, wrote movingly of the transformation that has taken place since it was left to the National Trust for Scotland. These have included 'motor roads', extensive new buildings within the bounds of the garden and some flashy new planting that is quite contrary to the donor's intentions. She concludes that it is time for the 'capital A of Art and Aesthetics to be given its rightful place before the big B of Business in the ABC of Conservation' in properties owned by the National Trust in England and the National Trust for Scotland.

Country houses have also aroused the interest of the commercial sector. There was a time when the only people who sought to make them a paying proposition were their owners, desperate to find a means of settling the bills. During the 1980s, however, country houses such as Alton Towers, Littlecote, Warwick Castle and Avebury Manor were acquired by entrepreneurs or companies specifically for the tourist revenues they could generate. The latest phenomenon is the emergence of pure landscape as a crowd puller. Landscape has literally become big business.

In twenty-five years the National Trust has succeeded in acquiring nine hundred miles of coastline, to protect it against commercial exploitation. In 1981, however, it was, unusually, outbid in its attempt to buy a coastal landmark: Land's End. Land's End is nothing except a piece of landscape which happens to be one of the farthest extremities of Britain. It is a wonderfully romantic spot, but possesses no history, famous building or national shrine to attract visitors. If the National Trust had succeeded in acquiring it, it would probably have demolished the existing hotel and other buildings. The London property company Regalian Developments had the foresight to realize that landscape-cum-heritage could be as good an investment as office blocks. The Trust offered £1 million, but was soundly beaten. The next year, in a private deal, Land's End again changed hands, being bought by Peter de Savary for a reported figure of £6.7 million. This enormous sum reflects the scale of tourist revenues that Land's End is expected to generate. Mr de Savary's confidence in the earning power of landscape can be seen in his subsequent acquisition of John O'Groats. It is also an ingredient in his plans for the stretches of Cornwall he has acquired around the little harbour of Hayle. At Hayle itself he has applied for permission to build 450 houses, maisonettes and flats, along with shops and health centre. Even critics acknowledge that the architectural calibre is high, but should it be there at all? The artist Patrick Heron, who was brought up in the area, sees the whole West Penrith peninsula going 'the way of the Côte d'Azur and the Costa Brava'. The irony, as he wrote in *The Guardian* in June 1989, is that developers like de Savary 'would not be in Cornwall at all . . . if those of us who live here had not preserved what he now seeks to exploit'.

Landscape is afflicted by the same dangers that threaten country houses. Over-visiting looks set to destroy the qualities for which we go there in the first place. Surveys show that most people's ideal is to find 'natural, unplanned countryside' in which they can enjoy themselves

as they like. They do not want interpretation centres or crazy golf. They want to get away from other people. Unfortunately, there are just too many people after the same thing. They are all so intent on escaping anything which smacks of organized recreation that, alas, they are apt all to find themselves in the same place. The most popular country pursuit is walking – after all, it is an almost universal skill. Tramp, tramp, tramp go the feet – so many pairs of them that the moorland in the Peak District and elsewhere is wearing out. For the first time in history scientists are studying how heather can be regenerated artificially.

Ironically the wildest, least polluted places are generally reached by means of the Great Contaminator, the motor car. Therefore the positioning of a car park becomes a major decison in the future of the landscape. Not to have a car park means that cars park just anywhere, blocking roads and disfiguring a valley. But when the National Trust created a car park at the foot of Stickle Ghyll in Langdale it proved so popular that the path up the mountain was immediately worn raw. The abrasion spread sideways to a width of twenty feet. To heal this wound the path was 'pitched', or laid with big, uneven stones in the manner of old paths used by packhorses; it is edged with boulders to discourage people from straying off it. Pitching paths such as this costs the National Trust £120,000 a year. Hauling the stones up on to the hillside is a major job. But nobody imagines that the pitched paths are anything other than an intrusion in the landscape, distressing for visitors and Trust alike.

What can be done to minimize the impact of so many visitors on our fragile landscape? Government ministers seem to believe that it is possible to redistribute the overload around new tourist sites. That is one of the reasons they are keen to develop tourism in the unlikely setting of industrial towns. But people who enjoy walking in the open air will not readily abandon it for the pleasure of going round old coalmines or woollen mills. They might, however, be persuaded to transfer their allegiances away from the most visited landscapes, if other parts of the countryside were made sufficiently attractive. Much more could be done to raise the visual quality of the countryside (through, for example, the ELMS agreements already discussed) in areas not in National Parks or officially designated as outstanding. Countryside rich in wildlife will also be visually appealing. In this the Farming and Wildlife Trust, formed twenty-one years ago, has set an outstanding example in showing how the improvement of wildlife habitats, including hedgerows, ponds, woods and unsprayed grass-land, can be combined with the demands of commercial farming.

Last year's winner of FWT's Silver Lapwing Award for farming and conservation, sponsored by *Country Life*, was John Berry of Billings-moor Farm in Devon, on the Duchy of Cornwall's Bradninch Estate. The first thing you will notice on visiting him is the large number of housemartins flying around the eaves of his farm buildings. Mr Berry has put up boxes for them and left an old pool from which they can collect their building material, mud. The hedges on his 232 acres are high and broad. Trees have been planted on every odd, unproductive corner of the farm, and three acres of new ponds have been dug. 'As a result,' wrote Robin Page in *Shooting Times*, 'an attractive landscape has been created, making a marked contrast to a farm across the valley, where the larger fields and low, short-sheared hedges appear to have very little of wildlife or landscape interest.'

Work of this kind does not require large sums of money. The Peak National Park has achieved wonders through its Farm Conservation Scheme, building twelve miles of drystone wall, maintaining ninety-two miles of the same, laying over three miles of hedgerow, managing and planting one hundred and eight acres of woodland and restoring ten ponds – all for pump priming grants to a total of £200,000. Already modest grants are available from the Ministry of Agriculture, Fisheries and Food to encourage hedgerow maintenance, stonewalling, heather regeneration and the planting of broadleaf trees. Recently the Countryside Commission announced a similar programme called Countryside Stewardship; in its first year it has been allocated £13 million. Conservationists have called for more farm support to be channelled towards the creation of attractive landscapes and good wildlife habitats. Almost certainly it will be so directed in the future; the only question is, how much? Britain could learn from the US policy of 'cross compliance', whereby the receipt of a whole range of Federal farm grants (including crop insurance) depends on the farmers' performance as conservationists.

There is no shortage of new directions to take. For example, the creation of new circuits of footpaths could be promoted. Britain is crossed by 140 thousand miles of ancient footpaths, many of which are rights of way. But tracks that were convenient for the ploughman or milkmaid of past centuries do not necessarily form attractive routes for the walker, which is one reason why so many footpaths are blocked. We need more new paths that are imaginatively routed for the walker,

while others will inevitably fall into disuse.

What must be resisted at all costs is the feeble-minded urge to clutter up the land with picnic tables, information boards and lavatory blocks, or the quest for 'unplanned' countryside will inevitably lead straight back to the landscapes that are already under strain.

The danger is that the tourist industry will spring like a hungry lion on to the back of any new region that attracts the interest of visitors. Decisions must therefore be made about whether tourism should be encouraged. If the majority of the nation does not want holiday villages built by Center Parcs, why on earth is the English Tourist Board permitted to give its largest grant ever (£1.5 million) to lure them to this country? The National Parks are already overcrowded, but the national and regional tourist boards continue to spend tens of millions of pounds annually advertising them. Regional tourist boards, two-thirds of whose funding comes from the subscriptions of their commercial members and their own commercial activities, are little more than trade organizations dedicated to furthering the interests of their members. Naturally they are unlikely to advocate restraint. Yet, despite their obvious sectional interest, they are regarded as having nearly a statutory role in formulating local policies on tourism.

The bias of the whole system becomes obvious when one considers that the funding of the ETB comes principally from the Department of Employment (because tourism provides jobs), and not from the Department of the Environment, as it should do if the ETB's role were really to manage tourism in the interest of the environment.

The first step towards solving the tourist problem would be to abolish the English Tourist Board and all the regional tourist boards in their present form. The money saved might be distributed among the three top tourist attractions which are charities. These are the British Museum, the National Gallery and the Tate Gallery. They rank second, fourth and sixth of all the most visited free attractions in Britain, yet their facilities hardly measure up to the 9.7 million visitors they annually receive. Rather than a non-elected quango such as the English Tourist Board, how much better it would be to have a Ministry of Tourism, such as exists in other European countries, which would be politically answerable for its policies. These might then be to control and manage tourism, rather than blindly promote it. At least one sound head in Westminster has privately suggested the setting up of an *anti*-tourist board.

The English Tourist Board already seems to have an inkling of which way the wind blows. *Investment in Tourism, January–June 1990* points to predictions that the real cost of travel could double over the next decade, severely reducing tourist demand. Fashion could swing against tourism. Because 'tourism is a polluter of virgin areas' it might become more chic to stay at home. 'In this regard, it may be worthwhile to consider the future effects of a development of a professional anti-tourist lobby.' It could indeed. Nothing is so vulnerable to the whims and vogues of the market as tourism. This makes it all the more urgent that we should not burden the countryside with permanent tourist facilities that one day nobody will want.

6

PLANNING BY TERROR

She did not know what to do.

I am referring, of course, to that early victim of the baby boom, the Old Woman who Lived in a Shoe. Britain's great baby boom occurred in the 1960s, being followed in the mid 1970s by a baby bust, in which the birth rate plummeted. Now, as the 1960s generation reaches the peak of childbearing age, the figures show a modest boomlet beginning to take place again. Since, in addition, the death rate has fallen, population numbers are slowly creeping up.

Britain's problem is therefore essentially the same as the Old Woman's, with one important difference. She found that her children would not leave home. Ours, it seems, cannot wait to get away and live on their own. Couples divorcing more frequently and the tendency for old people to live longer have also added greatly to the number of new households being created. Evidence suggests that many of the occupants of these new households expect to enjoy much more personal space than they might have done fifty years ago, when the population was considerably smaller. Yet England is already crowded.

She did not know what to do. Neither do we.

In particular, we do not know what to do with our land. We do not know which of many uses for it should be given priority. This is not very surprising because, unlike other European countries, we do not gather much information on how it is used at the moment. Our land is a finite resource – perhaps even, if sea level rises, a shrinking one. But we do not hear much talk from government about coherent policies on

England is ten times more densely populated than the United States. And three times more than France. And it supports more people per square mile than Japan.

how it should be used in the future. There is a simple reason for this: few such policies have been formulated. We have no national strategy for land use. There are intense rivalries between the various Secretaries of State who have a claim on the land. Transport wants it for roads. Defence needs it for firing ranges and training areas. Energy digs coal from it and builds power stations on it. Agriculture supports the interest of farmers, who actually work on it, even own it, but are allowed less and less freedom to do what they like with it. Environment seeks to protect it, but not too much, in case it discourages the house-builders. Trade and Industry wants more of it to disappear beneath factories, offices and almost any other kind of development that will make the country go with a buzz. They settle their claims with all the finesse of commuters jostling for the last seat on a train. When guile and determination fail, they resort to push and shove.

They like it like that, because they all hate planning. By the time the Conservative government came to power in 1979, planners had long been swallowed up in a tide of public rejection and hatred. They were held responsible for the rebuilding of British cities after the Second World War, nearly every example of which had been a catastrophe. They had once been the heroes of a new social order. Now they were seen as obstructive, arrogant, pettifogging, defeatist, callous, over-cautious and appallingly slow. The mechanisms for protecting the countryside had evolved slowly since the beginning of the century. The fact that they worked remarkably well was overlooked.

Planning incurred further odium as a brake on entrepreneurial creativity and the freedom of the individual. Consequently in 1980 Michael Heseltine, during his first spell as Secretary of State for the Environment, decreed that planners should have only a minimal role to play in controlling the visual appearance of new developments; that in future planning permission would not be needed for large numbers of relatively small household and industrial extensions; and that the old rules against 'non-conforming use' (which kept offices and factories out of residential areas, for example) would be weakened. Local plans were discouraged. 'Hitherto, there has been too much emphasis on restraint and restriction', commented the Minister for Local Government, Tom King. 'From now on, we intend to ensure that positive attitudes prevail.' Positive attitudes: a sinister phrase.

In theory, Britain enjoys a locally-based planning system. The strategy for a county is established by the county council, and the

It was exactly ten years to the day after the publication of the circular that Mr Heseltine returned to the D.o.E., and it is greatly to be hoped that this fateful coincidence will inspire him to undo his previous work.

district councils have responsibility for approving or refusing individual planning applications. The Department of the Environment keeps a watching brief on the whole process. For example, someone who feels that his planning application has been unjustly refused by the district council has leave to appeal to the Secretary of State. Equally, if the Secretary of State feels that a particular issue is too big for the district to handle, he can call it in to deal with himself.

A local base: such is the theory. In practice we have seen a succession of Secretaries of State for the Environment seizing district councils by the pigtails, pinching them and knocking their hats off. Despite the government's commitment to 'roll back the frontiers of the State', planning policy has become increasingly directed from Whitehall. The weapon by which this has been achieved is the planning appeal. Brandished over the heads of local authorities, it can be intimidating. Even the fact that the number of appeals by which the D.o.E. has overturned local authority judgements has nearly tripled, from 2600 in 1979 to over 7700 in 1989, does not reveal the full extent of central government influence. There remains the unknown but probably considerable number of cases for which planning permission was awarded because the local authority did not want to risk being taken to appeal. Appeals can be very expensive to local authorities, partly because of the uncertain question of costs.

Awards of costs, having risen progressively for a decade, soared by 65 per cent after the D.o.E. issued Circular 2/87 four years ago. In the early 1970s only some twenty-five awards of costs were made each year. By 1986–87 this figure had grown to 192, and in 1989–90 it stood at 344. Last year (1990) the National Housing and Town Planning Council issued a report on the subject claiming that, in addition, individual councillors might feel intimidated by the prospect of personal surcharges if they could be shown to have acted unreasonably. What constitutes 'unreasonable', the question on which many costs decisions turn, has not been adequately defined. As a result, the process is something of a lottery. What is more, local authorities are 6.5 times as likely to have costs awarded against them as developers.

The local authorities are also bullied through county structure plans. These are the documents in which county councils set out their intentions for the future. They can be amended by the Secretary of State. Recently he has been applying a kind of blackmail: do what you know I want or I will make you do something very much worse. Hampshire is a current example. With its motorways, fast trains, seaports, proximity to Heathrow, closeness to the mainland of Europe and – not least – fine landscape and attractive quality of life, it found itself at the epicentre of the 1980s economic boom. The housing stock had already expanded vigorously since the Second World War. Every decade from 1951 to 1981 saw a net increase of over 85,000 houses. Between 1981 and 1989 over 70,000 new houses were constructed.

The county council now believes that it is time to slow down. 'The vision driving the County Structure Plan is that of a prosperous county ... where the pursuit of economic growth is replaced by the desire to sustain what already exists. It is a vision of a County where the pace of change is slower than at present; where employers and employees feel secure; where the countryside is protected; where the identity of individual settlements is retained; and where infrastructure begins to catch up with the needs of local residents.' Wise words. Even wiser, it proposes that virtually no new green field sites should be made available for housing, other than those already identified. That still leaves room, Hampshire believes, for 58,000 new houses to be built before the year 2001. This includes the 31,000 for which planning permission has already been given and the 6000 already identified in the four local structure plans that have already been adopted. The remainder will come from the rebuilding of existing urban areas. At over 6000 new houses a year, the rate of increase would still be higher than that of any other county in the South East.

In ten years' time no less than 17.2 per cent of the South-East will have been built over, according to a recent government report Rates of Urbanization in England, 1981–2001. *In the North-West, the figure will be even higher: 21.6 per cent – more than one field in five. However, the Minister for Planning, Sir George Young, believes that these official statistics refute the claim that 'our countryside is disappearing under a wave of development'.*

But 58,000 new houses is 8000 short of the target for Hampshire set by Chris Patten, then Secretary of State for the Environment. This was identified by the London and South East Regional Planning Conference (SERPLAN) in 1989. Such is the fear the Environment Secretary can engender that the County Council's policy has been undermined by the Hampshire branch of the Association of District Councils. They have put forward their own figure of 64,000: because if the County Council's figure proves unacceptable, the Environment Secretary might impose his own. Neither the County nor the District council would be able to control where this extra new housing would go.

Terror is not the best method of ensuring the orderly development of anything. Certainly it is not the best method for achieving a balance of uses in our fragile countryside. Planning is like democracy. It has a myriad imperfections, but no one has yet thought of a better system.

But for planning to work, we must agree on our objectives. At a national level that means developing what we do not have at the moment: a strategy for land use. This will require the gathering of

information. A start should be made on those areas on the edges of towns and cities known as the urban fringe. The urban fringe is a twilight zone that is neither quite built over nor quite countryside. People from the towns hurry through it on their way to what they believe to be 'real' countryside beyond. What should be a resource we use with our usual extravagance and waste.

There has been much talk of new settlements: the government has even encouraged them through its discussion paper *Housing in Rural Areas*. So far every one that has been proposed has been rejected. The best places to locate such settlements would be on land which is already degraded, such as disused airfields. A national strategy for land use would help identify such sites. The same could be said of pleasure domes and holiday villages. If it is agreed that Britain wants these developments, some of which are on the scale of small towns, the planning system should take a positive lead in directing developers to the most acceptable sites. At the moment sites are only identified by developers seeing what they can get away with. This is enormously costly, not just to the local population, which may have to raise the money to fight an unsympathetic scheme, and to the government, which runs the public inquiry, but to the developers themselves, who are constantly preparing expensive proposals for nothing.

One factor that operates against sensible planning is the organization of Whitehall. The countryside falls between two Departments: the Department of the Environment and the Ministry of Agriculture, Fisheries and Food. The Department of the Environment is an immense, loose-limbed monster, responsible for everything from the poll tax to ozone depletion. Its staff has little expert knowledge of the workings of the countryside, for this has traditionally been the preserve of MAFF. In its own terms, MAFF has, since the Second World War, been astonishingly successful in promoting the interests of agriculture. Now that agriculture is in retreat, its staff lacks both the planning expertise and the necessary breadth of view to manage the diversified use of farmland. In the matter of food safety, MAFF has not managed to satisfy both the consumer and the producer, each of whom it is supposed to represent. So it is in the countryside: a public unsure of MAFF's stance on salmonella and listeria is equally sceptical of its attitude towards hedgerows.

This is the moment to reorganize departmental responsibilities and form a new Ministry of the Countryside, incorporating the old MAFF and parts of the D.o.E. One of its first jobs might be to regulate the government's own role as a consumer. In 1990 Professors O'Riordan and Weale of the University of East Anglia made the proposal that government departments, official agencies and local authorities should be made to account for their use of the environment, just as they would for other resources. In the countryside, this is an elementary principle of good planning that can no longer be ignored.

7

LOCATION AND LOCATION AND LOCATION: WHY THESE HOUSING PRESSURES?

Open the pages of *World of Country Homes and Traditional Living* – the monthly magazine everybody seems to be taking. We see a kitchen – the traditional country kitchen – which is only slightly smaller than a tennis court, its scrubbed surfaces soft with what appears to be a sprinkling of talcum powder. In the foreground, casually, as though just picked from the garden, is the wicker basket of carrots that Mandy, who styled the shot for the photographer, brought down from Fulham that morning. Over there, nonchalantly, hang a couple of old, very broad-brimmed straw hats, of the kind worn by retired museum directors in Tuscany. Well, it is a sunny day, or looks it, but of course the battery of lights and reflective umbrellas are out of camera. Actually, when the photograph was taken it was raining and Gurtz, the German photographer, had just been giving his slim young assistant, Mirabelle, merry hell for having left the extension wire at their last job in Cap Ferrat. None of that can be seen, however. On the printed page it looks a heaven of Englishness. 'Media personality Felicity Smyles brings the world of summer into her Gloucestershire home', reads the subhead.

The New Countryman loves to be deceived. He is willingly seduced by the endless stream of decorating magazines. The country look – a romantic jumble of rush mats and tattered curtains, faintly redolent of potpourri – has become so popular that unrestored houses attract, incredibly, a higher premium than restored ones. Naturally he wants to impart his own character to his newly acquired country place.

In the shire counties of England over 1,140,000 houses were built in the years 1981–88. In the South-West the rate of building went up by 55 per cent.

Naturally he wants to be a squire. The Home Counties have lost ground to the remoter shires, which apparently offer a more traditional way of life. He knows little about the country but all his fantasies tell him he will be happy there. Smart estate agents say that the new watchwords are 'quality of life'.

The trouble is that the New Countryman wants quality of life but does not want to pay for it. There are plenty of houses already in the countryside, but they have become expensive. Too many people are after them. Now the answer might seem to be to build more houses. That is what has happened over the past decade. But we know that this destroys the openness and tranquillity which attract people to the countryside in the first place. The position is hardly logical, but it would be a brave man who said, no, people should just expect to pay more for the privilege of living there. Yet why not? Oysters, being in short supply, are also somewhat dear. Nobody calls upon the government to increase production in the oyster industry. One does not absolutely *need* to eat oysters, that is true. But surely the countryside

is just the same. Many people would *like* to live there. That is a different matter.

Genuine need exists for a certain type of housing in the countryside. People working locally – either on the land or, for example, in a small engineering works – generally do not earn the kind of salaries that would enable them to pay the full market price for a village house. When cottages fall vacant, they are bought by weekenders and retirees. But if the lower-paid workers all drift away to the towns, where housing is cheaper, services also disappear. What the village needs is a permanent resource of cheap housing. Whisper it only, but this is another way of saying *council housing*. The stock of council housing has been depleted by the government's 'right to buy' policy. Housing associations do admirable work in providing rented housing but the Housing Corporation, which acts as their banker, has no money, having overspent on inner-city projects. Cheap housing holds little appeal for the private developer-builder, looking for profits. What is a cheap house? £70,000 may be half the going market rate, but a full mortgage for that amount will be beyond the purse of a couple each earning £2.50 an hour. We simply need more publicly-owned housing. Inter-war council estates, built on the edges of villages, often struck traditional country people as intrusive when they first appeared. Now nostalgia for them is growing. By comparison with what the free market has given us, they were models of good design.

Two-thirds of the houses that we now see disfiguring all areas of the countryside are large 'executive' homes. There is absolutely no need for them, in the strict sense. People in other countries – the Japanese are the obvious example – contrive to live in conditions that are far more circumscribed than ours. Japan is a crowded country but it supports fewer people per square mile than England. Such surveys as exist suggest that Britain's large new houses are often somewhat under-occupied. Hampshire County Council discovered that 60 per cent of new four- or five-bedroomed houses was bought by households of three people or less. Perhaps it is time that we revised our standards and faced the fact that aspiring purchasers of executive homes simply desire more space than the nation or the countryside can afford.

These houses are the ones that produce most profit, even though they satisfy a very small percentage of the market. The majority of new households being created consist of no more than one person. Already a quarter of British households are one-person, compared to an eighth in 1961. It is expected that between 1981 and 2001 the number of

In 1990–91 the total number of new rented and shared-ownership houses in villages (under 1000 inhabitants) subsidized by the Housing Corporation is likely to be about 400. Their rural programme accounts for a tiny percentage of their £1.1 billion budget.

The 1990 edition of Social Trends, *issued by the Central Statistical Office, states that, while the demand for housing is expected to increase over the next twenty years, it 'will change in its nature so that more, but perhaps smaller, dwellings are in demand rather than traditional family homes.' These are not the homes that, for the most part, have been built in the countryside over the past decade.*

Conservative politicians have not always been so cavalier about the landscape, nor so coy about putting a value on intangibles:
'It is the wealth and glory of England, this beauty which has been saved through the centuries. There could be nothing more disastrous, nothing more wicked on our part, than to waste it, to dissipate it, and to destroy in our profligacy a priceless and irreplaceable heritage.'

Stanley Baldwin, 6 July 1928

one-person households will have increased from 4.5 million to 7.1 million – 31 per cent of all the households in Britain. But moves by private developers to meet this demand are 'only limited', according to Surrey County Council. They go on building the same old executive homes.

The British are a self-effacing lot, always ready to see the other fellow's point of view. Consequently the exposure of what Nicholas Ridley described as the NIMBY – Not In My Back Yard – syndrome touched a raw nerve. He deplored the attitude that had already been summed up by his predecessor, Patrick Jenkin: 'I have a job; I have a nice house with a nice view; I live in a nice quiet neighbourhood; and actually I don't care too much if other people have not got jobs, or have not got homes at all.' But the sentiment that it is somehow embarrassing, selfish or wrong to occupy a nice house with a nice view rings hollow when uttered from the lips of a Tory Secretary of State. Certainly it is very far removed from the Victorian values applauded in other contexts. The sadness in life is that not everyone can enjoy an equally nice view. If you put your house in front of mine, you gain it, but I lose it.

Ask an estate agent which three factors most determine house prices and he is likely to say: 'location and location and location'. Everybody wants to live in the same place. There is a widely held view which says that, if planning restrictions were relaxed, house prices would fall. Not necessarily. Buyers will always fight to obtain a house in the 'best' area. Prices are conditioned less by the number of newly built dwellings on the market than by people's income and their ability to borrow money. Newly built dwellings represent only 1 per cent of the total housing stock and 10 per cent of properties on the market at any one time. When the Chancellor pricked the property bubble in 1988 it was not by releasing more building land, but by increasing interest rates. It would be all too easy to imagine from the high cost of houses that the South-East is experiencing a shortage of building land. Actually, the reverse is the case. 40 per cent more land has been given planning permission than has been identified as being required to meet housing needs in the various county structure plans.

We must wait until this 40 per cent has been built on before we give further permission to build. We must also think what, to successive Secretaries of State, has seemed unthinkable: that further permission may not be necessary. New studies suggest that we may have got the figures wrong. People have not behaved in the way that was predicted at the beginning of the 1980s. Households may not go on increasing at the rate we thought; in fact, after 2025 the total number could even fall. Who can tell whether these studies have provided more accurate forecasts than others? In the end we can only guess: there is no certainty about how people will behave, what they will want, whether or not they will chose to have families. It is outrageous folly to provide a supply for a demand that may never materialize.

Over the past thirty years the housing stock in Britain has increased by more than a third. Many of these new houses have been built in the countryside, but we cannot go on filling it up for ever. Not, that is, if we expect it to keep the beauty for which it is prized.

8

THE CRAMMING OF VILLAGES

Bad luck on the villagers of Sandhurst, a couple of miles outside Gloucester. In 1990 they were under water, when the Severn broke its banks. Traditionally, development in this area had been restricted because of the danger of flooding. But in the 1980s the pressure for housing became too great and the village doubled in size. Flood waters have been kinder than the developers. At least the flood waters go away; the speculative houses do not.

Even its admirers would not have claimed Sandhurst as anything special, it was just part of the traditional character of the English countryside. It used to be a scattered settlement. The fields came right into the centre of the village – or, rather, the village was dotted among the fields. All this has changed. The Gloucestershire structure plan, drawn up in 1981, smiled on village developments of up to ten houses. Ten houses would, in themselves, be quite a large number to add to a village all at one go. What the structure plan did not specify, however, was that *only* ten houses at a time could be so added. In too many villages, groups of more than ten have been allowed on appeal.

So houses marched into Sandhurst by the tenfold. A village of some fifty or sixty dwellings is set to become one of more than a hundred. In the past a village might have grown at a rate of a few new houses every ten years or so. A small number of houses – even ugly ones – could be absorbed as part of the natural evolution of the place. Even the most hardened NIMBYist would hardly feel entitled to keep the late twentieth century at bay altogether. But to have half the village built within a single decade throws it out of balance. However hard a developer tries to make it palatable, the lump is too big for the metabolism of an old village to digest.

Students of British architecture, go to Sandhurst! We all like to argue over the merits of Richard Rogers's Lloyds Building or Quinlan Terry's Richmond Riverside, but the real crisis in architecture is here. Like them or loathe them, Lloyds Buildings and Richmond Riversides are only one-offs. They are nothing compared with the hundreds of thousands of new houses on which no one seems to pass comment. These betray a level of national taste that makes us the shame of Europe.

The best new houses the Sandhurst example has to offer are in a kind of Kentish vernacular, wholly inappropriate to Gloucestershire. Inevitably, the houses are grouped round a cul-de-sac, which always looks out of place in a village, especially when it comes with the suburban panoply of curbstones and rumble strip. (The last, and a change in the colour of the tarmac, is a requirement of the highways authority: we would not want to miss the fact that we have passed from a maintained road to a private one.) And these are the *best*! The banality of the worst beggars description. Almost every one has what appears to be a submarine parked in the front garden. This is the propane gas tank, for which planning permission must, in theory, be obtained. Often the council will insist that it is screened, though this regulation is difficult to enforce and the screening usually takes the form of a hedge of cypress leylandii, as obtrusive as the object it seeks to disguise.

Expansion by groups of ten was intended to keep village services alive. Sandhurst gives the lie to this theory. Detailed consent has just been given to replace the village school with a row of six houses and build a further three on the playing field. The pub went the same way after the brewery sold it with a covenant that it should not continue in use as an inn. Five houses now stand on the site. This has been the experience all over Gloucestershire. In consequence, the County Council removed the group-of-ten principle from the draft of the revised structure plan which they submitted to the D.o.E. in December 1988. Chris Patten refused to accept this emendation. In March 1990 the document came back to the County Council from the D.o.E. with the group-of-ten reinstated. The county has been allowed to learn nothing from its own devastating experience.

This is infill. The prospect of whole new 'villages' being built in the

countryside generates such emotion that the idea of filling up the odd gaps left in old villages strikes many people, who do not realize what it means, as relatively benign. But infill, as it is being applied today, is really the most destructive of all forms of development. By the end of the century there will be few villages south of York that have not been affected and sometimes changed out of all recognition. The delicate fabric of a village can be ruined in just a few years.

The Picturesque movement bequeathed Britain a curse, and we are still living under it. This is the belief that buildings of different dates and styles will, once they are old enough, rub along together in mellow visual harmony. We relish contrasts; we have elevated mix-and-match to an aesthetic principle. It has dominated our planning policies since the Second World War. It has been the ruination of London. We must throw it overboard before it sinks our villages.

Infill cannot work, because the new houses are the wrong size. They are double-garaged executive homes (the garages indicate that the inhabitants are more likely to frequent the big Sainsbury's on the ring road of the market town than the village shop). Most old village houses are cottages, built in pairs or terraces, with only one or two gentry houses and a rectory dotted among them. Old cottages have low doorways and beams on which the unwary can bang their heads: their inhabitants would not forego them. When it comes to new houses, nanny is on hand in the form of the district surveyor to ensure that no one is exposed to such perils. This alone would make the dimensions of the executive home more akin to those of the rectory: and for any village to acquire ten, twenty or fifty rectories looks odd.

Most local builders, and even most national ones, are aesthetically all at sea, blown by the trade winds of their suppliers' catalogues and sucked into a whirlpool of visual reference supplied by *Dynasty* and the Costa Brava. However, there are quite simple rules for building harmoniously in rural areas. They concern the appropriateness of the material, the scale and the layout of the development. If these could be got right then style could indeed be left to the individual builder or householder – though more could reasonably be done within conservation areas to control details such as window frames and doors, where modern replacements are generally abysmal. Lower standards apply in the country than in London, even though the texture of a country village is often more subtle. When permission is given to fill a bomb-site in Pimlico, Westminster City Council insists that the style of the new build is exactly that of the Cubitt terraces to either side. Why need rural authorities be less rigorous?

It is time we asked whether the gaps themselves are mere dead space. The question is urgent, because before long they may have largely disappeared. Some of them have outbuildings – weatherboarded, weather beaten, ramshackle old sheds, which may make little commercial return but add their own note of rural informality. Others may be gardens; others still may indeed just be gaps, untended land hidden away behind a fence. One such site in the enchanting Suffolk village of Ufford is presently awaiting the result of a planning appeal. A new building here, just in front of the church and between cottage gardens, would dispel the magic of this perfect English scene. No doubt a certain number of village gaps could be foregone without loss of identity. But fill all of them, and the village will start to feel as crammed as a Strasbourg goose. It is in part the gaps which make the fabric of the village more open and relaxed than that of the town.

Not all examples of infill are bad. From the 1930s until his death in 1985 the unsung hero Frank Russell Cox showed that it was possible to build faithfully in the Cotswolds vernacular, at low cost and even using modern materials. A group of houses called Frogmeadow, at Dedham in Essex, designed by Raymond Erith and Quinlan Terry, demonstrates that even the most economical edge-of-village need not be devoid of architecture or charm. On the site of the old bailey of the motte and bailey castle in Eye in Suffolk is a circular development, with dramatic triangular divisions between the houses that also suggest fortification. It is a delight to discover this small masterpiece in a position tucked away from the rest of the village. Like much of the best village architecture ten years ago, this was financed by the local authority. Recently, some private landowners have helped lead the way. At Abbotsbury in Dorset, the Strangway estate provided land on which a housing association has built a stone-faced terrace of six houses. The architects William Bertram and Fell made it a model of its kind. Also in Dorset, Ken Morgan Architects have designed an equally remarkable thatched terrace at Sturminster Marshall.

In Ludham, Norfolk, an excellent development has just been built near the entrance to the village. It has a particularly interesting history. When Martin Walton, a landscape painter who lives in the village, noticed that planning permission was being sought, he went to see the plans at the North Norfolk District Council offices. They were for an uninspired group of detached houses. He thought something better was needed, spent time observing the local vernacular and then drew up his own scheme, in the form of a terrace with an arch through to garages behind. He gave this to the planners, and they suggested to the developer that he might well find it easier to obtain planning permission for the terrace than for his original proposal. He agreed, and had an architect draw up Walton's sketch. One feature in particular must have pleased him: it allowed two extra houses to be fitted on to the site.

But developments of this quality are, at present, rare exceptions. Designing village houses requires just as much imagination – and observation – as any prestige commission. For the most part, however, it is left to the local builder, who has no architectural training at all. Even this might not matter if the numbers were right. What we must not think is that infill can make a significant contribution to the total of new houses allowed for in country structure plans.

If we remain determined that structure plan targets should be met, other solutions must be found. One alternative that has been much canvassed is that of the new settlement, discussed in the next chapter.

9 _____

THE BLAND LEADING THE BLAND,
OR HOW TO ACHIEVE BETTER DESIGN IN NEW HOUSING ESTATES

The British are often said to be burdened with their past, and one way in which this is undoubtedly true is the unfortunate fact of our having invented the suburb. We were once a great industrial nation; the suburb came to be championed as the antidote to the dirt and overcrowding of the industrial cities. It became our forte. Foreigners greatly admired it, particularly at the turn of the century when the garden suburb movement attracted a cadre of idealistic young architects and horticulturists. At the time it seemed necessary and attractive. The trouble is that it escaped.

Just as rhododendrons sometimes escape from gardens and grow like weeds, choking other forms of plant life, so the suburb proliferated to such an extent that it is now just as much a menace as the industrial city used to be. The industrial city has disappeared; we have clean air, relatively (at least it is not laden with smuts). But our atavistic hatred of the city continues. The suburbs threaten to take over.

Even the design of our so-called new towns and cities is essentially suburban. This is a legacy of the garden city movement, of which Milton Keynes is the latest, and one hopes last, example. In its day the idea of Milton Keynes was nothing short of wonderful: a glamorous city centre, outlying sectors each with their own identity, their own sub-centres and points of interest, all lost (quite literally) amid the millions of trees newly planted on the gentle ridges of what used to be country hunted by the Heythrop. But then came the Oil Crisis and new feelings about energy conservation – and the brave new City of a

Thousand Roundabouts did not seem such a brilliant concept after all. The planners had made the fatal assumption that every inhabitant would drive a car. Such a dispersed pattern of settlement makes effective public transport an impossibility.

Nevertheless the horror continues. Milton Keynes still accounts for 1 per cent of all the new housing built annually in Britain. What have we learnt from Milton Keynes? Nothing.

The government has argued that new settlements are one way of meeting the predicted demand for housing. Since we cannot be certain about the scale of that future demand, we do not have to rush at the problem. This is just as well, because the number of new settlements that have so far scraped through the planning system is exceedingly small. Those that have won planning permission – such as the dreadful Thorpe Marriott, still being completed outside Norwich – are no more than agglomerations of speculative housing estates thrown together by the mass builders. The same is true of the three thousand house additions – to all intents and purposes new settlements – that have swamped old market towns such as Stowmarket. These examples, and

the plans of most new settlements now being planned, have all the faults of Milton Keynes with none of the advantages. There will be little to distinguish them from the suburbs of the 1930s, except this: they will not be attached to cities. They will sit on the countryside like a fried egg on a plate. We are on a course of civic and social disaster.

Generally, what are described as new settlements have few, if any, civic features such as public buildings, squares, or even shops. The principle of whether or not such settlements are needed has provoked fierce debate. But much less has been said of the housing estates of which they are composed – and which have been added to countless old towns and villages throughout the country. Yet most new housing estates are not only displeasing to look at, but use land with lunatic extravagance.

There are two main obstacles to sanity in the layout of housing estates: the shape of the roads and the form of the houses. They both add up to the same thing: density. Unless we contemplate building houses more closely together, with compensating areas of public space, we will never break free of the banality of the suburb. At the moment we are still back in the 1930s.

Before people or houses we have roads. Believe it or not, roads determine almost everything about the shape of a new estate. Official guidance on the subject comes in a deceptively mild-mannered document, *Residential Roads and Footpaths, Layout Consideration*, published jointly by the Departments of Environment and Transport. It sets out the rules which will enable car and lorry drivers to glide through a development with the minimum trouble or thought. This may seem a worthy enough ambition in itself. But should the convenience of drivers really be allowed to determine the quality of the surroundings of the people who live there all the time? Would it not be more sensible to make the development as inconvenient for drivers as possible, so that there are fewer of them?

Convenience for the driver means the following. Roads must curve. Houses must be set well back so that sightlines are preserved. Junctions must be round-shouldered, not right-angled. There can be no crossroads. No T-junctions. No Y-junctions. No traffic lights. No one-way streets. Cities such as Bath and eighteenth-century Edinburgh, which many regard as the most civilized urban spaces in Britain, would instantly have been rejected by the highways men. My dear Mr Wood, no Circus, I beseech you. We would have a forcible conglomeration of carriages within the hour. Och, Mr Adam, ya canna

have tha rood – Princes Street, d'ya call it? – all in a straight line. Gee
it a few kinks and a pimple roondaboot, mon.

Present highways regulations seek to remove all obstacles from the
driver's line of vision. This makes some sense for through-routes which
carry fast-moving traffic. It makes no sense at all for the centres of
towns and villages, where often the traffic will not move much quicker
than walking pace. A square is one of the commonest and most
satisfying of historical plan-forms. We must devise a system of regulations which makes the planning of new squares possible. The regulations should also concentrate on ways of forcing motor vehicles to slow
down – cobbled road surfaces are one solution – and not merely on
smoothing the driver's path.

The ordinary suburban house-type is fatal to good design. Detached
houses, all the same size, separated from one another by little gardens,
with garages placed prominently towards the street, become extremely
boring when built in large numbers. Individually they tend to be
pretentious, employing historical motifs derived from much larger
buildings. They mock the traditions from which their style is derived.
In groups they do not form interesting public spaces. Their isolation
one from another expresses their lack of community. Built of materials
transported from all over the country, they are the very emblem of an
energy-extravagant society. They also require perfect maintenance if
they are to last.

Worst of all, they squander the farmland on which they are often set.
Terraces of joined houses would be much more economical; they would
look far finer architecturally; they could be grouped around public

gardens that gave pleasure to everyone. Joined pairs of houses share many of these advantages. Even the Housebuilders' Federation recognizes the benefits. Nearly every illustration in *Good Design in Housing*, a discussion document which the Federation produced with the Royal Institute of British Architects, shows pairs or terraces of houses. The most expensive areas of London consist of little else. Yet speculative developers are intensely reluctant to provide them.

There has been much talk of a Classical Revival of late: the area of the speculative house is the one in which such a revival could do most good. The enormous advantage of Classicism lies, not in the fact that it can produce great buildings when handled supremely well, but in the general level of decency below which it does not fall when handled badly. Classicism is based on the repetition of elements, and some of these are commercially available already. Take the question of sash windows. It is quite possible to find adequate patterns among the standard ranges on the market – even some of the upright sashes in Magnet's Energy Efficient softwood 'Georgian' range are quite acceptable. To judge from other entries in the Magnet catalogue, however, this may be more by accident than design. The problem with the mass building suppliers is not that the product is fundamentally unsound, but that there is generally no architectural input into the design. Suppliers make the windows that they find convenient to make, not that suit the houses they will adorn. 'Theoretically a plastic window would be perfectly all right,' says the Classical architect John Simpson. 'You can mould it, detail it precisely, even incorporate double-glazing. The problem is that the people manufacturing them have no idea about history or design.' He goes on to say that in a large development there is no great economy in buying standard windows. Once the joiner has set his jig to the architect's specifications, he can run off windows for exactly the same price as those from the large supplier.

Unfortunately the neo-Georgian style, as seen on most speculative estates, is an abomination; it apes the superficial forms but not the proportions of Classicism. Who is to blame? The developer, the architect, the builder, the planner? All of them, perhaps. But the finger also points at us, the public. Today we make judgements of great aesthetic nicety in buying cars, but not in buying new houses. This may change. Architecture is given more and more attention in the press and on television. If developers find that the use of sound materials and the correct use of Classical proportions makes houses sell faster, speculative buildings will very quickly show the difference.

10

RULES FOR
DESIGNING NEW VILLAGES

*(Note: These rules can also be applied to
housing estates and even, sometimes, to
old villages)*

1. Do not call it a village, except in the unlikely event that it really is one. Most new so-called villages are the size of small towns, without a small town's amenities.

2. Confuse the highways engineer by asking him why roundabouts must be round. Say that you are designing ovalabouts or squareabouts. If you go armed with tact, charm, guile, bravado, patience and possibly a small bazooka, you may get him to deviate from the Highways Regulations.

3. Throw all your lollipops away. We have no need of culs-de-sac or turning circles.

4. No house is a kingdom unto itself. Though old villages are located in the country, they are generally quite closely packed with houses, and this is important to the identity of the place. Dwellings grouped or, yes, *joined* together can be made to form public spaces which have a value of their own. Historically, the most satisfying such spaces have been geometrical.

5. Convince your client that quality does not mean eight houses to the acre. Difficult, very difficult. Tell him that your village, if composed of terraces etc., will be described in *Country Life*.

6. Think very carefully about front gardens: many traditional village houses do not have them. Most developers automatically use wooden fences to separate one garden from another, but hedges would be much more attractive.

7. It is infinitely depressing if all the buildings in a village are the same height. Parish churches used to provide a moment of elation, their spires soaring above the surrounding cottages, but the Church of England is not anxious to take on any more. All new villages should have obelisks instead.

8. Even the smallest village must have a village hall. Village halls are still intensively used and new ones are frequently built. Civic buildings of this kind should be used to provide focal points in the plan; their architecture must express a sense of hierarchy. They can also give variety of scale.

9. There must be a shop. It will have to be prominently sited, at a place where customers can cross the road without incurring the wrath of the county surveyor. Specialist shops fare best, and this should be expressed in the shop front. If a sub-Post Office, commiserate with the proprietor over his need to install the official post office sign, which is a requirement of the job.

10. No garage should be visible from the street.

11. Hedges must not be cut down to provide lay-bys, as happens in many infill schemes. If the site already has hedges, lanes, field boundaries and monuments, respect them. Enhance them! These are the kinds of things that people come to the country for in the first place.

12. If the plan of the settlement is right, the design of individual houses can be left to the owner, within certain overall constraints. This will encourage diversity of style.

13. There must be a variety of dwelling types, which might include single-person flats, starter homes in terraces, pairs of villas, one or two substantial detached houses, sheltered accommodation around a court-yard. Most new housing estates are single class, single age group. They are monotonous and the inhabitants feel no sense of permanence, knowing that they will not stay there for long. If you provide a variety of different sizes of dwelling, people will have the opportunity to move on within the village, perhaps staying there for their whole lives.

14. Plant trees formally in the centre and luxuriantly on the edges. There are two kinds of village house: those with enough architecture to merit being seen on their own and those which take their character from being glimpsed between trees. The latter can be simpler architecturally.

15. Successful villages grow, but in order to prevent every green space being built over some might be designated common to all the village, protected by agreements under Section 52 of the Town and Country Planning Act 1971.

16. People who live in the countryside will want to get out into it. Try to establish a network of footpaths going out into surrounding fields which will give the inhabitants circuits to walk. Historic patterns of footpaths are not always suited to this purpose. One possibility is to have local farmers designate and maintain new footpaths under Environmental Land Management Services agreements (see page 24).

17. Use a computer to make the necessary calculations for the district surveyor. This is one advantage the Georgians did not have.

18. Pity James Gladstone. He attempted to do all these things at Upper Donington outside Newbury, and still his scheme was turned down on appeal.

11

HOME IMPROVEMENTS,
OR SOME EASY WAYS
TO HALVE THE VALUE
OF A HOUSE

The first thing the New Countryman will want to do on buying an old house in a pretty village is to undertake some home improvements. After all, why did he choose this particular house in the first place? Certainly not to let it stay the way it is. By the time he has finished it will be, as the estate agents say, 'fully modernized'. What they may not say is that, nowadays, everybody is looking for just what he bought: a place that has not yet been messed up. Yes, by his own efforts he will have so far improved his dwelling that it is probably considerably less desirable than when he started. So let's look at some easy ways of reducing the value of a house.

The essential first step is to drive to the local B&Q or Texas Homecare. These do-it-yourself supermarkets have been one of Britain's great contributions to Europe. Their counterparts in France and Italy have given Sunday afternoons a new purpose for the Latin male. He too has discovered, following British custom, that the best way to prove his manliness is by replumbing the bathroom.

Naturally the New Countryman will delight in the window section. The house he has bought is disfigured by having windows of different shapes and sizes. Over hundreds of years, starting in the sixteenth century, a succession of drearily cost-conscious owners employed the local carpenter to make small alterations to the existing fabric. This is part of the history of the house, which of course the New Countryman will wish to eradicate as soon as possible. Buy all windows the same size. Make sure that the frames are of that delightful dark coloured bongo wood – actually, any tropical hardwood from the rainforests will do. If he can only afford softwood, he must not think of painting it: he should have it stained to look like bongo! Painted window frames are absolutely *démodé* – which is hardly surprising, since they have been around for the last three centuries.

With any luck the windows the New Countryman buys will not fit the existing openings. This will give him the opportunity to knock down bits of the walls to get them in. Pseudo bow-windows will give an old-world look even to a building which is genuinely old.

The New Countryman will almost certainly find that his house has a perfectly serviceable front door. Let him throw it out immediately! The old door has the ridiculous drawback of being made of solid wood. This is extremely uninviting: it is as though the door were there to keep people from getting in. No, the New Countryman will be much happier with a door that admits light through glass panels. The smartest doors of all have a fanlight in the top. In the Georgian period the fanlight would have gone *above* the door, but the ceiling heights of the house are too low to take this. Never mind. Doors featuring what might be called the 'fallen fanlight' are notably more pretentious than anything the Georgians could have perpetrated.

Everyone these days laughs at stone-cladding, the fashion of five years ago. You know, the vertical crazy paving going up the wall, ha, ha, ha. But don't worry, because the New Countryman knows plenty of other ways to obliterate uneven wall surfaces, and all result in so mechanical a finish that in the end no one will ever guess the house had once been made by hand. For instance, the walls can be covered in cement render. Throw in some sand for added texture and the result can be every bit as pleasing as designer stubble.

In East Anglia, he must paint the stucco the colour of school knickers, a parody of the old Suffolk pink. Otherwise – and this is rather thrilling – he can remove the stucco altogether, exposing the half-timbered construction underneath. Ignore the fact that the timbers were never intended to be seen, or that piercing drafts will whistle through the cracks. 'Desolation shall be in the thresholds: for he shall uncover the cedar work.' Thus spake the Old Testament prophet Zephaniah, but who ever listened to *him*?

Now, you are probably wondering about the roof. It may be covered in mellow old tiles which have a bumpy surface; perhaps the roof ridge sags. These are signs of age which can easily be eliminated. The New Countryman can replace the lot with concrete tiles the colour of raw sheep's intestines. What is especially satisfactory about these modern roofing materials is that the vibrant colour will never weather down.

Particular thought must be given to houses that are one of a pair, or part of a terrace. Every New Countryman will want to know how he can most fully express his individuality. Here, satellite receiver dishes have opened up new possibilities. One of these cheerful status symbols can be guaranteed to catch the eye, even on the longest terrace. If the New Countryman prefers a more traditional approach, he should pay attention to his paint colours. Perhaps he shares a doorcase. Should his neighbour have his half painted, say, a subtle shade of maroon, why

shouldn't *he* freshen *his* side up with a vivid coat of turquoise? The contrast could be telling.

The garage can be quite a problem, unless the New Countryman has an old barn attached to his house. Then the answer is quite simple. Slam in an up-and-over door, and he can be sure that the house price will fall considerably.

There are many other tips I would like to give the New Countryman. Much can be made of sandblasting, both inside and out. Plastic downpipes show that he has brought his rainwater disposal system into the twentieth century. Chimneys are so easy to block up and remove that it seems a pity that the Young Fogey movement has caused a return to the open fire. The New Countryman will almost certainly find the existing chimneypiece too modest for his taste, in which case excellent neo-Adam styles can be obtained; the same goes for cornices and ceiling roses in easy-to-install polyurethene. The size of a small cottage should be doubled with a Crystal Palace-sized conservatory.

What, the New Countryman will ask, of listing, and conservation areas? Do these affect his freedom of expression? Let us take listing first. Fortunately for him it is the rarer of the two forms of official so-called protection. The estate agent will probably tell the New Countryman that the interior of his house is not covered by the listing regulations. This is not true, but since almost nothing can be done to enforce listing constraints inside the house, he need scarcely hesitate to throw out any uneven woodwork he may find – panelling, balusters or cupboards. If caught, he can plead ignorance. The Department of the Environment does absolutely nothing to warn the new owners of a listed building of their responsibilities.

Conservation areas are intended to preserve the other houses round about. Naturally the New Countryman will not want to think that the rules apply to him. But be warned: they do. He may be quite sure that, having been devised to preserve the most historically interesting and visually appealing neighbourhoods in the country, the powers of enforcement are Draconian. The New Countryman will be allowed to do nothing to his house without the most rigorous planning permission – except replace the roof, alter the windows, change the door, paint the whole building green, concrete over the front garden and add substantial additions to front and back. As you can see, the constraints are fearsome. It is greatly to be hoped you will not infringe them. The punishment for doing so is as ferocious as a gnat-bite.

12

THE FARMER
WHO PUT HIS LAND
UNDER HOUSES

Let me tell you a fairy tale.

Deep in the countryside there dwelt a farmer. This farmer was not a happy fellow: he complained bitterly about the state of the crops, the terrible drought, the terrible taxes, the rain during harvest, the townspeople walking dogs through his fields. Children, all farmers do this. But this particular farmer did have genuine cause to grumble, because the people of the town would not buy his food. 'No,' the people of the town would say to him, 'ships from across the sea come laden with mutton and butter, and it is a damn sight cheaper than the stuff you offer us.' That year the farmer did not trade in his Jaguar for a newer model.

But a war came to the land and all the ships were sunk. The people of the town had no food to eat, and the wise ruler said to the farmer that he had better do something about it. Suddenly the farmer became very happy. He ploughed, and he drained, and he sowed, and he reaped. His farm grew very big, and everybody thanked him, because it was wartime.

When the war finished the people of the town looked at his big farm and were none too sure about it. It was so very big, and not at all like the ramshackle old place they had known before. They thought the farmer was getting above himself. Besides, the ships with the mutton and the butter had started to arrive again. But the wise ruler, being a sensible chap and a bit of a farmer himself, thought differently. 'What if we have another war?' he said. So he turned to his chamberlain, whose name was Maffeking, and gave him bags of gold. 'Maff,' he said (for he enjoyed good staff relations), 'go to the farmer and help him make his farm the best and most productive that ever there was.'

And Maff did. And after twenty-five years or so every acre of the farm yielded 98 per cent more wheat. The cows gave 48 per cent more milk and the hens laid 52 per cent more eggs. 'Good for you,' said the wise ruler. 'If the people of the town had done as well, our economy would be stronger than Japan's.' The farmer bought not only the latest Jaguar, but a Mini for his wife.

Well, all went swimmingly for a while. But then the wise ruler started getting friendly with the wise rulers of all the neighbouring lands, and with their farmers too. Soon, do what they might, the townspeople could not eat all the food the farmer grew. (Which didn't make it any cheaper, but that's another story.) But the farmer went on growing it, piling the butter, beef and milk powder into mountains and making lakes of the wine. The wise ruler did not like this at all. But the farmer said, sorry, he could not turn the clock back, he could not stop it. The wise ruler begged and pleaded. The farmer still said no.

Then the wise ruler had a peculiarly brilliant idea. He passed laws limiting the amount the farmer could produce. He also paid him for leaving his fields fallow. The farmer found that he *could* stop, after all.

And he did not mind so much, because he had found a new crop which was much more profitable than all the old wheat and eggs and milk and barley. Buildings. They sprouted everywhere, going up like mushrooms. The farmer not only bought a new Jaguar, but hired a chauffeur and added a jacuzzi to the farmhouse.

He calculated that before long he would not have to farm at all. That was just as well, because soon most of his land would be under concrete.

But, children, here comes the interesting bit.

The funny landscape of beef mountains and wine lakes quickly vanished. And imagine the farmer's surprise when he and the townspeople woke up to find that they lived in a Greenhouse . . .

This is where life becomes too complicated for fable, because no one can predict for certain what the demand for food will be in thirty or fifty years' time. If scientific predictions are correct, British farmers on the whole stand to do rather well out of the Greenhouse Effect. The down side is that East Anglia may be lost under the sea. But other parts of the country could benefit from the warmer climate, becoming able to grow a wider range of crops than before. There is talk of lemon groves in Kent and fields of nodding sunflowers in Berwickshire. The uplands in particular will become more productive. Everywhere, the presence of more carbon dioxide in the atmosphere could actually help stimulate plant growth.

The outlook for farming in other countries is far less rosy. Sadly, those which at present have most difficulty in feeding themselves are likely to be worst affected. Areas in which agriculture is now marginal will become desert. Population growth will exacerbate the shortages, and famine will stalk the land. Even highly productive regions like the Great Plains and Corn Belt of the United States, on which much of the rest of the world relies, could be adversely affected. A doubling of carbon dioxide in the atmosphere, causing a rise in temperature and fall in soil moisture, could cut yields by between 10 and 30 per cent.

The world's population stood at 3000 million in 1960, at 5000 million when the Brandt Commission reported in 1981, and is predicted to rise to between 8000 million and 15,000 million in the next century.

These areas, like other parts of the world, will probably experience disruption from the increasing occurrence of what at present seem climatic freaks – violent storms, excessively long droughts, unseasonal frosts. It is estimated that food exports from the US will fall by as much as 70 per cent.

No doubt there will be increasing pressure for favoured countries such as Britain to do their best to help feed the rest of the world. Naturally they will only do so if the rest of the world can afford to pay them for what they grow. This could be a problem. But who knows? If Thailand and Indonesia repeat the economic miracle of Taiwan and Singapore, their inhabitants might expect a richer diet. Perhaps the people of Poland, Czechoslovakia and Hungary, having reorganized their industries, will also find that they can afford to buy more food from abroad.

Not that growing food for export will be the only demand on Britain's land. A proportion of it will no doubt be used for raising the new crops that will provide fuel and plastics-substitutes when the oil runs out. Agricultural priorities will change. The discussion will no longer be about surpluses but about a return to full production.

And now, imagine the farmer in my fairy tale. What will be his reaction when he looks out and sees that the fields which used to grow crops have been covered with houses? He will scratch his head and stamp his foot, but he will never be able to farm them again. He – and the rest of us – may well look at the profligate, wasteful developments sprawling across the land and weep. 'If only I had not built over my land', the farmer will say . . . But he has done so, and now it is too late.

However, this is not a fairy tale, and there is more than one possible ending. Imagine that the present trend towards vegetarianism continues, and virtually everyone stops eating meat. All Britain's pasture land could be given over to the growing of lentils and pulses – new, genetically engineered strains which are highly productive. Imagine that the agriculture of the USSR and the former eastern bloc countries becomes as efficient as that of Lincolnshire. This may be hardly credible at the moment; certainly the problems of investment in such a diffuse industry will be greater than those of refinancing a single factory. Yet it is not beyond the bounds of possibility. Imagine, finally, that the Intergovernmental Panel on Climate Change has got it spectacularly wrong. The fact that the six hottest summers on record have all occurred in the 1980s is nothing more than an astonishing coincidence. Motor cars are banned and all the chimneys in China capped with mufflers to clean the smoke. The farmer could then go back to complaining about the rain during harvest, and life would continue much as before.

The trouble is that nobody knows which of these endings is the most likely one. But anyone who wants to be sure of living happily ever after should not take a chance.

Do not build over farmland. We may need it.

13

WHY A BARN CANNOT BE A HOUSE

One benefit to the landscape must emerge from the change in agricultural priorities. It is no longer possible to argue that maximizing farm production is so vital to the national interest that the construction of new barns and other farm buildings should stay outside the planning system. Some new barns are as big as factories, but outside the National Parks they can be put up anywhere, entirely without planning permission. Even within National Parks the planners do not have the power to stop them being built, merely to advise on siting and design. The exemption applies as much to a fish farm, complete with security fences and floodlighting, as to more traditional farm structures. Intensive agriculture is not so different from other industries, so why should it still be a case apart?

Manufacturers do not seem to give much thought to minimizing the impact of new agricultural buildings on their surroundings. They do not vary the standard designs to acknowledge regional traditions. They do not use local materials. They do not attempt to camouflage the huge roof surfaces, which now flash in the sun, by painting them dun-colour. A model for the design of sympathetic new barns is provided by the National Trust's work in the Lake District. Carefully sited, they are faced with boulders and roofed with stone slates. Their cost – between £40,000 and £50,000 each – could not be commercially justified by the rents of the farms, but the Trust's example could still have a wider application throughout the country if a suitably encouraging grant system were worked out. After all, capital grants from the European Community helped fund the erection of the ugly shed-like barns that went up in the 1970s. As a quid pro quo, farmers would have to accept that their buildings became subject to planning discipline.

Old barns have become another planning anomaly. If they are listed, they are all the more likely to be destroyed. Why this paradox? Because a listed barn will receive the necessary planning consents for being converted into a house far more easily than any unlisted building. Indeed, through the Trojan horse of barn conversion, developers can infiltrate houses into areas of the countryside in which no new residential building is normally allowed. The policy that a redundant listed building should be found an alternative use generally overrides other planning priorities. Often planners feel unable to refuse listed building consent because they fear that a refusal will be overturned on appeal. Yet, in nine cases out of ten the listed barn loses most of its character through conversion. Consequently, some local authorities are now deliberately refraining from listing important barns because they know that it would increase their chance of being wrecked. The scale of the problem can be seen from the fact that Essex alone has over a thousand listed barns.

A barn which has been converted to a house may or may not form an attractive building in its own right. But one thing is for sure: it is no longer a barn. It is impossible to live in a barn without inserting windows. Arguments may vary as to whether these are best provided by dormers or by the dreaded Velux roof-lights that are the plague of so many historic buildings: but windows of one form or another will have to go in. The internal space – perhaps majestic – will have to be divided. Since barns do not have chimneys those, too, may be added. All this comes on top of structural repairs that can lead to the renewal of nearly every visible part of the building. In the case of the timber barns of East Anglia, both clapboard walls and thatched roof will be replaced, leaving only the timber frame original. It can be done well or badly, but do not call the end result a barn.

It would be bad enough if the alterations stopped with the structure. They do not. Habitation brings with it cars, garages, patios, sun umbrellas, washing lines, carriage lamps and swimming pools. In other words, the surroundings of the building change completely. What had previously seemed unkempt and disregarded becomes, by comparison, hyper-tidy and obsessively manicured. Style in these matters must always be a question of personal choice. The point to be made, however, is that the old rural feeling is lost. Imagine the impact on the Yorkshire dales if each field barn (there is one literally in every field) had been turned into a weekend home? The great farmsteads of Devon present another problem. They are so large that they can be converted into as many as two or three dozen dwellings. The newcomers swamp the little hamlets, of perhaps only half a dozen houses, to which the farmsteads are attached.

In the heady days before the property collapse barn conversions enjoyed a considerable vogue with the public. In 1988 the estate agents Cluttons reported that 'the demand for converted barns is now so great that they are being snapped up within days of being put on the market and prospective purchasers are having to outbid each other.' It is not unknown for unlisted barns to be lifted up from one county and put down in another, where the speculative builder can work his magic. The *Country Life* property correspondent described just such a converted barn on the village green at Datchworth in Hertfordshire, for which offers of around £700,000 were sought in 1988. Now there are signs of disenchantment on the part of buyers. Many conversions were to conspicuously low standards, and barns which are part of farmyards do not offer the privacy that people often seek in the country. But the practice goes on. In the Welsh Marches, estate agents' windows are full of derelict barns for sale, with and without planning permission, at prices over £100,000. To many people's surprise two applications have been made to Caradon Council in Cornwall for the conversion of barns to executive housing, which the Council commendably refused. The applicant was our conservationist Prince of Wales.

It sometimes happens that a historic barn is de-listed after conversion because the work has so thoroughly compromised its original character. In May 1990 English Heritage issued a statement urging local authorities to introduce a strong general presumption against residential conversion of listed barns, but this lacks statutory authority. It is undermined by the D.o.E.'s draft Planning Policy Guidance note, *The Countryside and the Rural Economy*, which proposes removing the restriction whereby only barns that are redundant may be converted.

Undoubtedly the best use for old barns is for them to stay in agriculture. The farmer's objections, though familiar, cannot be ignored. Old barns do not always take very large machinery, they can have awkward spaces, they are not necessarily in the best place on the farm, and they require frequent maintenance. The last point did not matter when there was a large number of men on the farm: mending roofs gave them something to do during the winter. Now repairs are an unwelcome extra cost, and one that is often neglected. Even the Society for the Protection of Ancient Buildings is prepared to admit that, given a straight choice, a new farm building is likely to be more convenient than an old one.

Recently, however, it has come to be seen that old barns still have many practical strengths. Such has been the rate of agricultural change that some of the purpose-built pig units and other plant that went up in the 1970s have themselves become redundant. They are so specialized that they can only be demolished. Traditional farm structures, on the other hand, are more flexible.

There are many ways in which a barn can still fulfil a practical role on the farm. Barns were originally built for storage, and this remains one of their most satisfactory, if least glamorous, uses. At Holkham in Norfolk the eighteenth-century barn by the great Samuel Wyatt has been converted to a grain store. An Oxfordshire granary now serves as a pesticide store. Forklift trucks which turn on a sixpence can overcome the difficulties of restricted space, making it possible to stack sacks of fertilizer, chemicals or animal feed on pallets. Unsightly modern silos can be placed within old barns and thus removed from view. Thatched and stone-walled buildings have excellent properties of insulation which make them ideal for fruit storage and even, in some cases, the keeping of livestock such as suckling calves and turkeys. They are adaptable to specialist uses like potato-chitting – bringing on shoots under artificial light – or cheese-making. The working life of an old building is sometimes prolonged by the addition of a new one alongside: an example where this has worked well is Quatt Farm on the National Trust's Dudmaston estate in Shropshire. Encouragement has recently been given to those wishing to keep old barns in agricultural use by MAFF's imaginative Farm and Conservation Grant Scheme. Under this, farmers can obtain 35 to 50 per cent grants towards the repair of vernacular buildings which are kept in agricultural use. So far the total of grants paid has been modest: £600,000 between February 1989 and September 1990. But the Scheme is an encouraging indication of MAFF's belief in the contribution that attractive buildings and environment can make towards the future prosperity of farmers.

The Rural Development Commission gives grants for the conversion of redundant farm (and other) buildings. They have helped small businesses making such diverse products as saddles, beeswax, model trains, furniture, church organ pipes, bows and arrows, and soft toys. Several micro-electronics firms operate from converted barns; so do garden centres and gymnasia. All these uses are friendly to the buildings in which they operate. They have also proved economically viable. But whether a use of this kind will seem attractive to other farmers will largely depend on how much money they think they can realize by selling the barn for other purposes.

The first thing that must happen is for planners to abandon the notion that a residential barn conversion saves a historic building. Indeed, it is time that a moratorium was declared on all conversions of listed barns into houses. Perhaps we must steel our hearts and accept that a certain number of barns must be allowed to crumble gracefully into extinction. This would be a sadness, but surely better than seeing them destroyed through conversion, while suburbanizing the country-side to boot. Tougher policies on planning permission would reduce the market value of barns, making other uses seem more competitive.

14

SUBURBIA IN THE COUNTRY: SWIMMING AGAINST A RISING TIDE

The countryside is suffering death by a thousand cuts. We have so far lost our sense of what is appropriate, not to mention our gift for designing the small things in life, that every day the country-side comes to look a little bit more like a suburb. This is in part a reflection of the changing character of the 'rural community'. Indeed, that phrase is becoming increasingly defunct. Country dwellers no longer form the cohesive community they might have thirty years ago. What is more, fewer of them could be called rural. Who is the countryman these days? Agriculture employs only a tiny percentage of the working population. More and more, the people who live in the countryside do so because their offices have relocated, or because they commute two hours each way every weekday, or because they have snapped up a second home at an affordable price, or because they have retired to what they regard as tranquil surroundings. So too the planners. For planning is a mobile profession: promotion generally entails a change of scene. Consequently, ambitious planners do not always possess an intimate knowledge of the locality in which they operate. They themselves may well be new to the country. The result is an increasing penetration of urban, and suburban, values.

Does this matter? If the people who live in the country are the same as those who live in the suburbs, is it not logical that the one should resemble the other? Well, yes, it may be logical, but fortunately logic has almost nothing to do with decisions that we take about either our personal appearance or the look of our surroundings. The most

When all our roads are
* lighted*
By concrete monsters
* sited*
Like gallows overhead,
Bathed in the yellow
* vomit*
Each monster belches
* from it,*
We'll know that we are
* dead.*

John Betjeman,
'Unexpensive Progress',
Collected Poems, 1958

important thing is that, when they affect the countryside, these decisions should be actively made. We must not allow ourselves to float into them unawares.

Street lighting has been one area of drift. We have been carried along by the spring-tide of the council lighting departments: left to themselves, they would have every village in the countryside lit up like a television studio. Added to this, the Freight Hauliers' Association has long campaigned to see street lights installed along the full length of all the trunk roads and motorways in the country. Yet everyone knows how loathsome it is to walk out at night and see the horizon disfigured by the orange glow of distant sodium lights. (Astronomers, prevented from seeing the stars, have particular reason to hate it; they are campaigning for Dark Skies 2000.) One of the charms of visiting Eastern Europe after *perestroika* has been to discover that the pall of suburbia has not yet descended. People are expected to take sensible precautions – carrying a flashlight, for instance – when they roam abroad after dark.

Why do we accept these disastrous levels of lighting? In places where lighting really is necessary, are there no ways of mitigating its impact? Of course there are. Lampposts do not have to wave over the road like tall trees. Where the A40 passes Northolt Aerodrome, in Ruislip, the lampposts are about half their normal size, little more than a dozen feet tall. They light the road perfectly well but the glow is far less visible from a distance. Light which is directed downwards on to the road is likely to reflect back up into the sky. Recently the London Borough of Wandsworth has been relit with lamps set at an angle to the road. What is more, their light is pink rather than orange.

Now, consider the lamppost itself. When it is doing the job for which it was intended, lit up at night, its structure can hardly be seen. But in daylight hours it is all too visible. What thought do lighting engineers give to the contribution their lampposts make to the rural scene? Little, to judge from the ugly structures they choose. But lampposts need not be hideous, angular things, made of cast concrete. The Victorians designed charming lampposts, as could some architects and industrial designers today. Good design need not add to the cost. The trouble is that most of us are too prepared to put up with easy, fifth-rate solutions. It is time that we insisted on higher standards from our local authorites. If we did, we might find the local authority perfectly willing to help. Recently Cambridgeshire County Council gave every assistance to Houghton and Wyton parish council when it paid for some excellent new, locally-made street lights to be installed in the village. Parish councils are empowered to raise money through the community charge for improvements of this kind. Fortunately not all villages find it necessary to have lampposts. A cheap solution is among the least obtrusive: attaching lamp-brackets to existing buildings. It would be even cheaper, of course, to have no lighting at all.

Street furniture is a recent cause for concern, largely because there is so much more of it about than there used to be. In past centuries the only items of street furniture in many parishes were the horse trough and the stocks. Now the idea has grown up that 'heritage' locations are somehow incomplete without a clutter of unhistoric intrusions – signs, kiosks and the like. The first rule governing street furniture should be to have as little as possible.

In previous generations, when much street furniture was still a novelty, distinguished architects gave thought to humble or utilitarian structures. Sir Giles Gilbert Scott won the competition to design the red telephone box. Sir Edwin Lutyens designed bus shelters in Northumberland, and the early electricity pylons – 'nude, giant girls', the poet Stephen Spender somewhat extravagantly called them – owe their shapely curves to Sir Reginald Blomfield. As late as the 1950s Grey Wornum, President of the Royal Institute of British Architects, designed lampposts for Westminster City Council. Today this is rarely the case. Most street furniture is now bought off-the-peg, not made in the locality, perhaps even designed overseas. The result is to replace British regional accents with a kind of visual Eurospeak. The French company Decau is now marketing circular drums, topped off by an onion dome, to local authorities in Britain, to whom they offer an unsuspected source of advertising revenue. Such drums or kiosks, poster-plastered, are the very hallmark of Paris. If bought, they will sound an obviously false note in any British market town. The mystifyingly sophisticated Superloo – French again – was in the vanguard of the foreign invasion.

Yet street furniture is one part of the visual destiny of a village over which its residents have a large measure of control. In many cases it is selected and paid for by the parish council. What is more, perfectly good examples of bollards, benches, tree grilles and the like can often be bought from manufacturers' catalogues, for little extra cost. In some cases the additional expense will be a good investment. Cast iron bins not only enjoy a much longer natural life than those in fibreglass, but they can withstand even the toughest vandal's boot. Above all, a village with carefully chosen street furniture will look infinitely better than one with a clutter of poor quality examples.

A word of caution must be expressed about manufacturers' catalogues. Some simply do not contain any satisfactory standard ranges: others present the good alongside the atrocious. A little research, aided, perhaps, by the conservation officer of the District or County Council, will lead you to the most promising. The 'Guildford', 'Hindhead' and 'Merrow' bus shelters made by Astolat Co. Ltd of Peasmarsh, Surrey, cannot be praised too highly. Made of wood, they have overhanging roofs supported on timber braces which recall the Surrey vernacular so much admired by Lutyens. Dorothea Ltd of Buxton, Derbyshire, have specialized in reviving the tradition of cast-iron street furniture, making tree grilles, bollards, benches, brackets, railings, lampposts and an unusually fine range of litter-bins. They also make some free-standing structures, such as band stands. Broxap and Corby of Manchester also manufacture admirable cast-iron pieces (though I am less convinced by the wooden benches and litter-bins in their Countryside Collection).

Unfortunately, there are one or two types of street furniture for which no adequate design yet exists. Virtually all the huts bought for car park attendants are, in the words of one English Heritage official, 'pre-cast plastic horrors' supplied by a single North of England manufacturer. Even English Heritage buys them, because there would appear to be no other standard range. Bottle banks are becoming more common, but is the inevitable green bin appropriate for a prominent village location? Again, little choice is available. Visually, the Superloo rarely enhances the village scene, though it is becoming increasingly commonplace. If one really is considered essential, it should be located so that it is not visible from the street.

The removal of street furniture can be just as disturbing as its insertion. Even in conservation areas, street furniture has no protection unless it is specifically listed. A small change in the law, bringing street furniture within conservation area legislation, would have prevented the worst excesses of British Telecom's appalling campaign to replace the red telephone box. Council lighting departments are liable to act in just as high-handed a manner as Telecom. They have no obligation to consult locally when replacing lampposts not actually owned by the parish. The Norfolk village of Wymondham has been a recent victim. The highly active Wymondham Heritage Society is understandably incensed that no one outside the County Council had prior warning of the deed. Highways departments are notorious for the abandon with which they strew village streets with yellow lines and obtrusive signs. Villages require a different treatment from Oxford Street. In narrow lanes the presumption against parking is self-evident. Smaller signs – or even one sign at the beginning of the village – would be enough, if the restrictions were properly enforced.

At the very least, the parish council's powers should be enlarged to ensure consultation by the public utilities before changes are made. They can already exercise some influence, when they know in advance what is happening.

The low quality of much of the detail of the countryside can be avoided. There is no absolute, God-given reason why grit bins need to draw attention to their presence through being coloured a plangent shade of yellow. In Herefordshire, for example, they are grey. Grass verges do not need to be lined with curbstones, nor trimmed to billiard-table smoothness. The more enlightened councils have already recognized that cutting should not take place before early summer, to allow the wildflowers to seed. With imagination (admittedly not its

most obvious characteristic) British Telecom could even reduce the impact of telephone wires on our villages. This will become an increasingly urgent consideration, as fax machines and telephone-linked computers become commonplace.

Concern for appropriate street furniture must not be confused with a Village of the Year mentality, obsessed with tidiness. Often the country is not a tidy place, and attempts to make it so do not always end happily. Tall do-it-yourself fences around a cottage garden, shielding domestic life from the road, are entirely out of place. One of the things that make villages different from towns is their openness.

Unfortunately, the Government has itself been one of the worst suburbanizers, through the privatization programme. Old fashioned public utilities, such as the Post Office, tended to have a high sense of their responsibility to the public in terms of design. Alas, the alien-looking new telephone boxes which have already blighted large areas of the countryside show just how dangerous a newly privatized industry can be when it is in search of a new corporate image. British Telecom may now sponsor an Environment award, but it has done more than most bodies to promote the suburbanization of rural England. We wait to see how the fledgling independent electricity companies will assert their individuality – perhaps through eye-catching new junction boxes and space-age substations.

15

ANCIENT AND MODERN: THE CHURCH IN THE COUNTRYSIDE

For the stone shall cry out of the wall,
and the beam out of the timber shall
answer it.
Habakkuk, 2:11

From the Revd. M. Gargoyle,
The Rectory,
The Church of St Scudamore,
Lesser Piggott.

Dear Parishioners,

Let me begin my first contribution to St Scudamore's parish magazine by passing on to you the thanks of Father Lacey-Cuffs for the really charming present you gave him on his retirement. His love of the rectory garden was most thoughtfully recognized in the sun umbrella and patio set, and I have no doubt that Philomena and he will soon find just the place to put them. The very handsome window-boxes adorning their flat at Eastbourne suggest that their horticultural ambitions will be given fuller rein ere long.

I am sure that you shared my emotions on
hearing his final sermon on the text of
Isaiah 13, 21—22: 'Their houses shall be
full of doleful creatures; and owls shall
dwell there, and satyrs shall dance there.
And the wild beasts of the islands shall cry
in their desolate houses, and dragons in
their pleasant palaces: and her time is near
to come, and her days shall not be
prolonged.' Ah, yes. The playful allusion
which this allowed him to the state of the
rectory is yet further evidence of the
sparkling humour for which he will be long
remembered.

At least in one respect the era of
modern comfort has arrived at St
Scudamore's. The carpet for the nave,
expected next week, will make the old church
cosier than it has ever been.

Yours cordially,

Mike Gargoyle

Dear Parishioners,

The visit of the surveyor produced exactly
the result everyone had been anticipating:
the rectory is in such a bad state of repair
that it will have to be sold. The rural dean
tells me that to him this comes as no
surprise whatever — indeed, predicting just
this situation, he stopped spending money on
its upkeep long ago.

The surveyor says it could be turned
into flats, with one for Flo and me. I will
not hear of it. The rectory is far too

prominent and imposing in the village for
the likes of us. My idea is for the clergyman
to live in exactly the same way as his flock,
not to pretend he is setting them an example.
Besides, the dignified, solid old building
sends out quite the wrong signals about the
present state of the Church of England.

    Turning to the church, we hope that the
installation of the lavatories by the
transept will transform this time-worn
edifice into a truly multi-purpose resource.
It is amazing how an inconvenient old
building can sometimes be adapted to serve
today's social needs.

Yours cordially,

Mike Gargoyle

Dear Parishioners,

Flo and I are looking forward to moving into
the new parsonage, just as soon as the
concrete parking area has dried. We are
particularly pleased to have selected this
model from the Church Commissioners' green
book on the design of parsonages. It looks
similar to the builder's houses recently
erected on the site of the church hall, sold
last year — except that the parsonage is only
one storey, of course.

    At last we feel that we have a late
twentieth-century home from which to conduct
a late twentieth-century ministry, sharing
the same values as everyone else. We are
looking forward to inviting you all to join
us there for a glass of Flo's homemade cider
very soon.

You will all be pleased to hear that the last of the pews was removed from St Scudamore's in the course of this week. Several people have commented on how practical the new stacking chairs are.

Yours cordially,

Mike Gargoyle

Dear Parishioners,

I would like to propose an addition to our Sunday services: namely, that we drink a cup of coffee together afterwards. This would celebrate the feeling of togetherness which is of course the prime object of our worship. I have viewed with admiration the kitchen and adjacent committee room that the Vicar of St Tote's, Punter's End, has created inside his church.

The older among you will remember Father Lacey-Cuffs' regular port-and-stilton parish luncheons in the church hall. That hall certainly proved to be an asset. Even the rural dean was surprised by how much it fetched as building land. St Scudamore's Close, the development which replaces it, really is most attractive, if perhaps more conventional than the conversion of the old church school house that took place last year.

Yours cordially,

Mike Gargoyle

Dear Parishioners,

Thank you all for your attendance at our
little evening. I can only apologize to
those who were not able to get in, but, as
you know, our bungalow is only a fraction of
the size of the old rectory. I was touched
that some people took the opportunity to
remind me of the happy church evenings held
there by Father Lacey-Cuffs, but we must all
move with the times.

The crush inspired me to ask the rural
dean about new community facilities in the
church. Imagine my surprise when he told me
that so much money had been raised by the
sale of the church hall that we can actually
build quite a large extension. There has
already been some discussion as to where
this extension should go. I realize, as one
of you pointed out, that the churchyard
occupies several acres, but we would not
want to subject our old folk to a walk of
what could be as much as fifty yards,
especially as the flagstones are not
absolutely flat. Everything for convenience
is my motto. No, it must be a new structure
attached directly to the church itself. We
might even think of knocking down the old
porch which is leaking; it has already
served out its useful life.

Can I advise the carpenters among you
that we now have a goodly supply of seasoned
oak for sale? The old pews were really quite
substantial.

Yours cordially,

Mike Gargoyle

Dear Parishioners,

Discussions about the extension proceed
apace. The architect favours one abutting
the tower. No medieval structure would have
been built in this position, so the new work
could not be mistaken for anything other
than a building of our day and age. This will
of course be reflected in the style, though
in order to satisfy English Heritage bits of
flint will be pushed into the concrete to
make it tone in with the existing walls. I am
told that if the new rooms form an extension,
rather than a free-standing structure, we
will not have to pay VAT, which is another
argument in its favour.

    The architect has also suggested that a
car-park would be a major benefit, and how
right he is. Happily there is plenty of room
to construct it in the churchyard. This will
provide an added spur to tidying up the
gravestones, which, I am sure you will
agree, give an unfortunate impression of not
having been touched for centuries.

    You will be interested to know that our
old pews are now in the Raving Bonkers
Discotheque, who have also opened
negotiations for some of the stained glass.

Yours cordially,

Mike Gargoyle

Dear Parishioners,

At last work on the extension has finished.
Our parish discussions will now take place
in the atmosphere of a true conference

facility. The first meeting of St
Scudamore's Finance Committee took place
there last Tuesday. It was altogether a most
agreeable occasion.

Like some of you, I had not expected the
car park to take up quite *all* the churchyard
but one day the parking space for 250
vehicles will come in useful.

Yours cordially,

Mike Gargoyle

Dear Parishioners,

Everyone is so pleased with the new
extension that I have decided to hold next
Sunday's services there instead of in the
church, as it will be much warmer. I propose
that the congregation gather around the
conference table. For this one occasion we
can use the movable hostess trolley as the
altar.

So, see you in the lounge.

On Tuesday evening the Sunday School
will show slides of their Club 18—30
pilgrimage to Marbella. This takes place in
meeting room 1. In meeting room 2, the
Mothers' Union will debate the topic 'Aids
and the communion cup'. The bell-ringers'
practice has been postponed. Since the
proposal to allow a mullah to call the
faithful to prayer — a most imaginative
example of inter-faith *rapprochement*, in my
view — still causes controversy, this will
be discussed in meeting room 3. Meeting room

4 will be occupied by the church organ committee, considering the offer Metal Tubes Ltd have just made for the old pipes. No point in keeping them now that our services are accompanied by guitar!

Yours cordially,

Mike Gargoyle

Dear Parishioners,

Our services in the new extension have indeed gone well. Everyone enjoys the light, airy atmosphere, and the central heating has certainly proved efficient. This was the final encouragement that I needed to dispense with my old robes. I feel so much closer to the congregation in a simple jacket and slacks. The padded vinyl banquettes thoughtfully provided by the architect are indeed practical.

Following my lead, the parochial church council has decided that we can now dispense with the old St Scudamore's altogether. Negotiations are therefore under way to sell it to a life assurance company. Personally, I can imagine no more appropriate use. Much more sensible to make proper provision for the future than to trust in providence. In the modern world, there are limits to how far we can stretch our faith in God.

Yours cordially,

Mike Gargoyle

16

THE FARMER'S CURSE, OR DON'T FORGET THAT THE COUNTRYSIDE IS LARGELY MAN-MADE

I went by the field of the slothful, and by the vineyard of the man void of understanding; And lo, it was all grown over with thorns, and nettles had covered the face thereof, and the stone wall thereof was broken down. Then I saw, and considered it well: I looked upon it, and received instruction.
Proverbs, 14:30–32

The cry goes up: Farmers Bad, Nature Good. Farmers are fast gaining on cowed and humiliated architects as the country's most hated professional group. This is very convenient for their critics, most of whom live in towns, but ignores the fact that many of our most treasured landscapes are not the product of untrammelled Nature, but of Nature interfered with by man. Stand at the head of Monsaldale, one of the most famous views in the Peak District. In prehistoric times the hillsides would have been wooded. Man came and cut down the trees. (Evidence of this early period of occupation can be seen in the Iron Age hill fort on Fincop.) Such woods as one now sees were planted by the Duke of Devonshire about a hundred years ago; these are now reaching maturity and will soon be felled. For the most part the hillsides are bare, having been grazed by sheep for centuries. They were even balder at the beginning of the century, when sheep farming was more profitable. In parts the scrub is starting to reassert itself, and it must be periodically removed if the scene is to remain recognizably the same. Striding along the bottom of the valley is a railway viaduct, against which Ruskin fulminated. Now even this, long since closed to trains, has come to seem an inalienable part of what many people would regard as a 'natural' landscape. In reality, it is no more natural (if by that we really mean 'primeval') than St James's Park.

Man drained the marshes, built the dykes and created the shallow lakes that together make up the subtle beauty of the Norfolk Broads: indeed, the lakes are the result of what now seems the undesirable practice of peat digging. The New Forest, planted for the benefit of the Norman kings, was very far from popular with the local inhabitants when it was established. If it had not been for the great flocks of sheep that once grazed southern England, our downland would not have been created. We may rejoice in the possession of specially designated Areas of Outstanding Natural Beauty but, strictly speaking, the term 'natural' is a misnomer. Except for river estuaries, there are almost no true wildernesses in Britain.

We now live in a 'leisure' countryside. It is not protected for the sake of food production, but for itself. This leaves us with a substantial problem. The landscape people wish to see is the one with which they are familiar. But it will only stay that way if it is farmed. Should farming cease, much of it would revert to unattractive scrub. Ultimately the scrub might grow up into forest, but the landscape would not remain the same. The National Trust has faced this problem in the Chilterns and the Thames Valley. Where farms are untenanted because of the poor return from the land, the Trust has had to resort to a peripatetic flock of sheep, bussed around the country to keep the landscape in good repair. Where grazing by cattle has receded, the landscape has become colonized by bracken, among whose many evil properties is that of being a carcinogen. Now, if the countryside is to be farmed profitably, can we stop it changing? The answer to that question is no.

For half a century the nation has been trying to preserve the traditional landscape of the uplands – areas such as Exmoor, Dartmoor, the Yorkshire Dales and Moors, the Lake District and Snowdonia. Were it not for government and EC grants, nobody could make a living from farming in these remote, austere places. Even so, upland farmers are not insulated from developments in the rest of the industry. Economics are forcing them to keep bigger and bigger flocks, even though the farmer's labour force – himself – has remained

Well over 80 per cent of the British countryside is farmed.

constant. Breeds have also changed. On Dartmoor the familiar suckler cow used to be the hardy little Galloway but, as Sir Derek Barber, former Chairman of the Countryside Commission, recently explained, this has been superseded:

> Galloway dams are replaced by Friesian crosses to bring more milk into the calves now sired by big Continental breed bulls. The tenets of economic efficiency are thereby observed as larger, more profitable stores travel off to the markets.
>
> But bigger cattle require more food in winter, so the tractors with their loads of silage go off to the moor. Sometimes it is very wet, so deep ruts appear and frequently the loads are discharged near the gates, where long-term damage can be done: mud and its associated appearance offend the tourists, on whom much of the local economy subsists.
>
> The solution is the offer of a financial agreement, by the park authority, to persuade the beef-store producers back into the traditional breeds, where the damage to the face of the land would be less acute. But how far down this road, away from advancing technology and the market economy, is it defensible to proceed? Where is the threshold point before the farmers themselves are dressed up in smocks as a tourist attraction with, one might say, Alton Towers coming to Dartmoor?
>
> 'An Obsolete Future', *Country Life*, 28 June 1990

Surely the British public is too independent and sophisticated to wish the countryside to be preserved as an elaborate contrivance. However, if change cannot be held at bay on Dartmoor, one of the most sensitive, intensively visited and grant-supported areas in the country, what hope for the rest?

Actually, considerable hope. We cannot stop the countryside changing, but fortunately not all recent changes have been for the worse. Some people think that a field of oilseed rape in flower – a dazzling yellow block on a background of dun and drab – is a fine sight. You don't? Be thankful, then, that less rape is planted now that the subsidies have been reduced. Perhaps you felt nostalgic at the disappearance of the haymeadows. Who could have predicted that, with the growth of 'horseyculture' and organic farming, they would be coming back? Or that cornfields would once again be flushed with the red of poppies? Having been widely grown after the Second World War, linseed more or less disappeared, but has recently staged a return. There cannot be many people who regret the appearance of its light blue flower, unexpected though it is. The same might be said for borage, daffodils or any one of a host of 'alternative' crops. The increased profitability of running a pheasant shoot (thanks to corporate entertaining) has benefited wildlife, if not sport: what is good for young pheasants is also good for many other species of bird. So far has the property market changed over a decade that farms with a good house, hedgerows, woodlands and wildlife now possess a higher capital value than those whose landscape was denuded in the 1970s.

Indeed, one of the greatest present threats to the beauty of the countryside is not from too much farming, but from too little. Rank with weeds, the fields taken out of production through set-aside will not strike many visitors as pretty. Certainly they inspire gloom in the heart of the countryman, who knows that the weeds will soon colonize neighbouring land.

Crops come and go. More permanent fixtures like hedgerows tend only to go. Some are being replanted, supposedly at only about half the rate of those being removed. It is said that we end every year with two and a half thousand fewer miles of hedgerow than at the start. If this is true – and it is almost impossible to substantiate – it would be a large figure. However, since the total length of hedges in England and Wales is estimated to be three hundred thousand miles, enough to stretch three times round the world, we would still have quite a lot left. The annual rate of loss would be under one per cent. What we must ensure is that the hedges which disappear are those we can most easily spare. The enormous hedgerows flanking a medieval drove road or marking a parish boundary must be defended at all costs; they need protection by the Landscape Preservation Orders which the present government (in National Parks at least) has a pledge to introduce. However, the large numbers of hedges planted as a result of nineteenth-century enclosures may not be historically important or species-rich. They may not make as telling a contribution to the landscape as, for example, a new hedge planted along a ridge. Change, even in the sensitive realm of the hedgerow, is not always forever or for the worse. Consider the case of Town Fields outside Aldford, on the Duke of Westminster's Eaton estate in Cheshire. Originally a medieval village open field, it was enclosed in the nineteenth century, no doubt in the face of fierce opposition, then 'unenclosed' when the hedges were removed ten years ago, arousing equally strong feelings. Now, as part of a policy to

enhance the landscape quality of the estate, it looks as though the hedges will go back. Enclosure again!

It is widely recognized that we must have more farm woodland. But we should also be agreed on the need for more forests. Once most of lowland Britain was covered in forest, but we cut it down, sometimes as recently as the turn of the century. At present Britain imports 90 per cent of timber products from overseas. This costs us more than £7 billion each year. Such is the public opposition to new forests that the Forestry Commission does not believe that it will ever be able to supply more than 25 per cent of home demand. The increase will be caused only by the growing up of plantations which have already been created. Where is the rest of our timber to come from? Other countries may not always have surplus timber to supply us. The task of persuading underdeveloped countries not to destroy their rainforests will become more difficult when they realize that we are not prepared to see new planting to replace the forests which we ourselves have felled.

In Britain the area of land covered in forest – about 10 per cent – is well below the European average of 25 per cent, despite the fact that British trees grow better than those of many other countries.

New forests are urgently needed, if only so that we can play our part in countering the Greenhouse Effect. We ought to enjoy them. Walking in forests can be more interesting than plodding across an endless expanse of open moor – certainly the Germans, brought up on folk-songs and Schubert *Lieder*, think so. They and the people of other foreign countries actually seek out forests as places to holiday, much as we formerly sought the seaside. All right: let's not have conifers imposed on the landscape in mathematically shaped blocks as they were after the Second World War. Fortunately the Forestry Commission adopted a more sensitive approach to design years ago. But there will still need to be some planting of conifers, if only to act as a nurse for the other species.

Outrage! There is a vocal body of opinion which seems to regard Douglas fir and other 'exotic' conifers, which, fortunately, grow well in soil that has been already impoverished by man, as only slightly more friendly to the environment than napalm. The popular prejudice against almost any form of forestry runs high. It does not always run true.

In December 1990 the Countryside Commission began planting a New National Forest around the ancient forest of Charnwood in the Midlands. This process could take up to half a century to complete, for the eventual size of the forest will be that of the Isle of Wight. The trees, most of them broadleaves, will not be continuous: blocks of them will be scattered among the existing towns and villages, covering only half the land area within the forest boundary. The blocks will be carefully designed to include rides and glades, to encourage wildlife. Let us hope that the example of Charnwood New Forest will help us overcome what amounts to a national phobia against forestry.

There is much to be gained by our becoming more sophisticated consumers of the countryside. Some changes are inevitable, and there is not much point in trying to obstruct them. What we *can* do, however, is to ensure that the modifications to our landscape which are bound to come in one form or another do not cause a loss of quality. The new landscape will be different from the old, but there is no reason why it should be less beautiful.

Most changes in farming have this overwhelming merit: they are reversible. For the really evil men of the countryside we must look to those people whose destructive acts last for ever.

17

ELYSIAN FIELDS: HOW THE COUNTRYSIDE PARADISE CAN BE REGAINED

T he media have an appetite for bad news. This is as true of the countryside as of anything else. But the countryside is fortunate in that many of the errors of the past can be put right. It all depends on whether they have involved bricks and concrete. Landscape that has been built over is unlikely to recover its former beauty. Landscape that has not been put under roads and buildings can be restored. It might seem to some romantic purists that restoration, requiring a conscious act on the part of man, is a somewhat artificial process. They should think back to the eighteenth century, when many of our finest landscape parks were being planted. Those landscapes were nothing if not contrived, but that does not diminish our pleasure in them today. What is more, once the first steps have been taken it is surprising how quickly Nature spontaneously asserts herself. Create the right conditions and long-dormant wildflower seed bursts forth, apparently from nowhere. Half an acre of meadow can quickly attract a colony of butterflies, even when no butterfly can be seen on the surrounding prairie fields.

Charles Flower knows what can be done. For five years he was director of the British Trust for Conservation Volunteers, overseeing four or five hundred local groups across the country as they busily coppiced woodland, mended footpaths, restored sand dunes, layed hedges and cleared riverbanks. Since 1986 he has been what he describes as a 'grower'. He has a 170-acre farm at Shalbourne outside Newbury, most of which is farmed by a neighbour. On the rest he has a haymeadow, a hazel coppice and a business growing wildflower seed for sale. He also acts as a consultant, advising landowners on how they can enhance the beauty of their fields.

There are many ancient coppices in Britain but, come the spring, few will be carpeted with primroses. Once they would have been. Traditionally, coppiced trees were cut down at the base every half a dozen years or so, in order that the thin, supple branches could be used for sheep hurdles, bean poles or thatching spars. They were then allowed to grow up again, spreading outwards, until the process was repeated. With the disappearance of the demand for hurdles, the trees went uncut. They grew tall and dense, keeping light from the woodland floor. Result: many fewer wildflowers. Over the past ten years Flower has been patiently re-coppicing his trees, carrying on the work started by his father-in-law after the last war. He has had to educate himself in the technique of layering – persuading a tree to extend itself

laterally by burying a mature shoot in a trench. This increases the density of the hazel and so helps defeat the brambles that would otherwise take over.

Cutting the hazel has let in the light, and now the woodland floor is thick with primroses and violets. Flower says that now 'the number of species of trees, shrubs, wild flowers, mosses, liverworts, lichens, fungi, birds, butterflies, moths and all other insects must come to well over five hundred'.

The coppice gives no commercial benefit: even firewood is all too plentiful since the storms of 1987 and 1990. This is not the case with another landscape feature whose reinstatement Flower has been encouraging: the haymeadow. Within the space of one generation haymeadows have all but disappeared. After the Second World War progressive farmers planted rye-grass to improve milk yields; then, in the 1970s, some stopped mixed farming altogether, switching entirely to arable. The haymeadow, occupying an odd, damp corner of the farm, had a purpose when there was stock to graze it. When the stock had gone, it was drained and brought within the rest of the farm. But fashions in farming change; so do farmers' perceptions. Those with cattle or horses might well remember the haymeadow with something more than nostalgia. As Flower says: 'People with old haymeadows have lower vet bills and produce very high quality milk.'

The old Berkshire meadows supported an enormous number of plant species. It is known roughly what they all were, and consequently Flower does not believe that his artificially sown wildflowers will disturb the ecology of the area if they are based on appropriate species. He admits the danger. As he puts it: 'People like me have the potential to muck things up hugely, particularly in a Site of Special Scientific Interest.'

Flower also helps manage Snelsmore Common, on which he happens to hold long-disused commoners' rights. Commoners stopped grazing their cattle on the Common a century ago. As a result, scrub steadily encroached on the open heather until it was on the point of taking over completely. Gradually, Flower and his team have been liberating the heather. 'We've been at it for seven or eight years. Every time a patch of heather is cleared we get another pair of nightjars – there are presently five or six pairs on the Common.' Trees are left in clumps and belts to help absorb the large numbers of people who now visit the Common, run by Newbury District Council as a country park.

Planting trees, laying hedges, nurturing chalk grassland, rescuing a water meadow from dereliction – by these means Flower has prevented some landscape features from disappearing and introduced others from scratch. Three lessons emerge from his work. The first is that conservation of this kind is more likely to happen in a prosperous countryside than in a destitute one; often the worst enemy is neglect. Lesson number two concerns government grants: relatively small amounts of money can achieve great things. But, for them to be effective, landowners and farmers must know what historical features are to be found on their land and what things it would be appropriate to restore. Landscape and conservation surveys are therefore a pre-requisite, which should be encouraged through the grant system. The third lesson is that even a small area of meadow, even considerably less than an acre, can attract a large number of species. Nothing is too small to start on.

18

THE MOST PROTECTED,
THE MOST AT RISK:
THE NATIONAL PARKS

What do we have instead of strategic planning in Britain? We have something called the Sieve. It works like this: would-be developers put the map of Britain on the Sieve and rattle it around. Gradually all the Green Belts, Sites of Special Scientific Interest, Environmentally Sensitive Areas, National Parks, Areas of Outstanding Natural Beauty and so on will be seen to slip like sand through the holes. What is left will be ordinary, four-star Britain. 'Can't be good for much if it isn't protected', they tell the public inquiry into the new warehouse development-cum-nuclear waste disposal centre.

'But this is a completely unspoilt stretch of countryside', say the local residents' committee, struggling to meet six-figure legal costs. 'It's beautiful.'

'Sorry, can't be. Not protected.'

The developer who manages to identify a beautiful unprotected site near a motorway, preferably in a sparsely populated rural area where there are not many inhabitants to complain, stands to make a bonanza. Why not? Such are the rules of the game under our imaginative system as presently operated. The only people who lose are those wanting to live in a countryside that retains some of the qualities of the Britain in which they were brought up.

But a funny thing is happening in all those areas that have dropped through the Sieve – the so-called protected areas. If we look at them carefully, we find that they are not as protected as we had thought.

Take the National Parks. They comprise areas such as Dartmoor, Snowdonia, the Derbyshire Peaks and the Lake District which everyone agrees are of supreme landscape beauty. Being designated as National Parks is a kind of official recognition of this fact. Arguably these are the most beautiful landscapes in Britain (as National Parks are chosen for their wildness, contenders in the south of England – notably the Downs and the New Forest – have been excluded). There are also no National Parks in Scotland, where, instead, the great landed estates have done the job of preserving the landscape very well.

Now, since so many people want to live, holiday or weekend in beautiful countryside, it follows that the pressure to have the National Parks covered in time-shares, holiday cottages and leisure complexes is intense. If they are so covered, the landscapes will be less beautiful than before. Then, according to the theory of *laissez-faire*, the developers and holiday makers will move on somewhere else. Possibly. But what *laissez-faire* does not take into account is that beautiful landscapes are not endlessly renewable: in absolute terms the nation will have suffered an irreparable loss.

In theory, development is controlled more rigorously within the National Parks than elsewhere. In practice, it once was. The government even intends that it still should be. The plain fact is that it isn't. New developments may not be so big as elsewhere but, amazingly, there are proportionately more of them.

Both the number of planning applications received and the percentage for which approval is given have risen to dizzying heights. For this we must thank the development and tourist industries which are making our leisure time so much more comfortable and fulfilling. They are doing particularly fine work in the Brecon Beacons. It may be one of the quieter Parks, but still they have managed to double the number of planning applications within the space of a single year. In the Lake District, half the planning decisions by the National Parks authority taken to appeal are being overturned by the Secretary of State for the Environment.

There was a time when 50 per cent more planning applications would have been rejected in the National Parks than elsewhere. Probably even that statistic conceals the fact that many developers would not have dared make an application in the National Parks because they knew in advance that it would get nowhere. Now the number of refusals within the National Parks is very nearly the same as outside. And the total number of planning applications received has gone up by over a third. Soon the much-abused army firing ranges will be the only wild places to have escaped development.

Irony of ironies! The 'positive attitude' introduced by Michael Heseltine and his ministers in 1980 was meant to stop at the boundaries of the National Parks. The Parks and other protected areas were specifically exempted from the new ruling that development was to be considered a good thing unless proved otherwise. What happened in practice? Precisely the reverse. As the Council for the Protection of Rural England observes, 'the National Parks relaxed development control standards *more* than did planning authorities in the wider countryside'. Why? Because, like everyone else, they could hear the tumbrels of the appeals system rolling. Institute a Terror and you can never be quite sure how it will turn out. Ask Robespierre.

Deeds count more than words. Whatever the government may say about the National Parks is outweighed by what it does. Consider the case of the bypass considerately provided for the little Dartmoor town of Okehampton. When the bypass was first envisaged, as long ago as 1968, the Department of Transport proposed a northern route, avoiding the Dartmoor National Park. That same year a local railway line closed, so didn't it seem sensible – from Whitehall – to run the new road along the site of the old tracks? This new route went south, not only through the National Park but through the medieval deer park of Okehampton Castle. The public inquiry which took place in 1979 lasted ninety-six days and it was a mere three and a half years before the Secretaries of State for Transport and Environment announced their decision: in favour. Such was the opposition that the case rumbled on, being examined in 1985 by a joint committee of MPs. They too found against the southern route. Again, these advisors were overruled. Surprise, surprise, the bypass now goes through the Park, despite the availability of an alternative.

The Okehampton bypass is just one example showing that the government does not regard National Parks as inviolate. Talk of a new East Coast motorway, part of whose course would run through the North York Moors National Park, would have been unthinkable before Okehampton set the precedent. A bad winter could resurrect the many-times-buried idea of a cross-Pennine motorway linking Manchester and Sheffield, through the Peak District. Surely there must be

The Peak National Park is visited annually by twenty-one million people – ten times more than visit Yellowstone in the United States. This makes it the second most visited National Park in the world, after Mount Fuji in Japan.

The National Parks Review Panel, in its excellent report of March 1991, urges that the Parks should actively promote 'quiet enjoyment and understanding' on the part of their visitors. This would mean banning noisy and intrusive activities and encouraging visitors to take pleasure in the tranquillity and remoteness which the Parks were formed to preserve. The Parks need a new act of Parliament enshrining this principle. They need it now.

some areas of the countryside which the government hold to be sacrosanct? Do we need a new designation, awarding completely untouchable Crown Jewel status to the very finest of the fine?

The polluter pays. This is an accepted principle in industry and agriculture, and it must be extended to development. The National Parks urgently need an obligatory development tax. This will be no substitute for the strictest planning controls, but it will help take the steam out of the market. One of the greatest problems of the National Parks is the sheer number of people who visit them. There must also be a tourist tax, charged on accommodation, which would provide revenue to restore those areas damaged by excessive visiting. This was recently proposed in the Lake District but, after fierce opposition from the local tourist board, the National Park authority withdrew the idea. Why listen to the local tourist board?

Unfortunately the tourist tax would not reach everyone, since the majority of visitors to National Parks are day trippers. Is it time to charge admission? Surely people would be prepared to pay to enter National Parks, if they knew that the money was going towards maintenance and conservation. Visitors readily pay to enter the National Parks of the United States, where they were first introduced, and of Canada, which has the greatest area. The problem is that in both these countries the land of the National Parks, being virgin wilderness, is entirely owned by the state, whereas much of the land in the English and Welsh National Parks is privately owned and supports a local economy.

Consequently, the best ways of controlling access must be the simplest. Ban cars. Close certain roads. Impose ferocious parking restrictions and tow offending vehicles away. Make people walk to the places they have come to enjoy. Naturally, special buses would have to be provided to give access to the infirm and the disabled; in areas where the experiment has already been tried, the first to approve of the closed roads policy have been wheelchair users, who can use hard roads without fear of being knocked down by motor vehicles. Most National Park authorities are prepared to consider only repairing the damage caused by over-visiting: hardly ever does one hear proposals which would actually discourage people from coming in the first place.

19

CONCLUSION

I have tried to show why to go on building in open countryside would be disastrous. The farmland that seems surplus to requirements today may well be needed by future generations: no one can predict for sure what demands the fast increasing population of the globe will make on the available food resources, or whether large acreages of land will need to be given over to the growing of crops for the biomass fuels that one day may replace oil, or whether the Greenhouse Effect really will confuse the geography of the planet, making Britain more productive but turning parts of the Mediterranean countries into desert. There can be no certainty as we peer into the future. This makes it all the more important to keep options open.

No certainty. But there is one prediction about which almost everyone agrees: it would be foolish to depend entirely on the continued existence of the motor car. Yet that is precisely what we must do if we go on scattering new dwellings and settlements around the countryside, making efficient, economic public transport an impossibility. Fortunately the countryside is not the only place where new dwellings, if they are needed, can be built. Large areas around our towns and cities have already been built over, but these suburbs make a wasteful use of space. Their leafy streets can be attractive, but large detached and semi-detached houses are not particularly ideal for two critical sectors of the population, the young and the old. The young are frustrated by being so distant from their friends and the excitements of the town. The old feel isolated, being far removed from shops and the hum of life. Both groups would benefit if parts of the suburbs were redeveloped to higher densities – that is to say, with people living closer together. This would create a greater sense of cohesiveness. It would bring to the suburbs some of the civic amenities of the town. It would satisfy the predicted future housing demand, which is overwhelmingly for one-person households.

There is another point which receives almost universal agreement. Building over the countryside is ugly. Fortunately it is not inevitable that the countryside should become increasingly degraded. Often the qualities which we now miss in it can be restored. Leisure and tourism are putting immense pressures on the National Parks, simply because

the National Parks have done their job well and preserved the beauty of our most outstanding landscapes. Enhancing the beauty of over-looked areas of the countryside might help defuse the threats pre-sented by the leisure and tourism industries. Too many people all going to the same place can cause erosion: the countryside wears out. But a greater problem than the visitors themselves are the buildings that the leisure and tourism industries construct to take profit from them. The need for a strong planning system, capable of saying no and meaning it, has never been greater.

The countryside is money. Consequently, the interests seeking to develop it are financially formidable. However, the power does not lie all on one side. Ordinary people can still hope to exert influence if they go about it the right way. The first thing that is necessary to making one's voice heard is understanding how the planning system operates. I hope that the next chapter will go some way to giving you this golden key.

20

RULES OF ENGAGEMENT

What can the individual do about it? Some people may be surprised to discover that there are actually plenty of opportunities for them to make their views known, both when the general strategy for the planning of their area is being established and when it seems to them that something has gone wrong. Planning is about agreeing priorities and achieving a reasonably just balance between the interests of different members of society. Consequently no one can expect that his or her opinion will prevail on all occasions. But people who do not take part in the process at all cannot be surprised if the outcome is not the one they would like.

The first section will describe the different levels at which planning decisions are made. The second section provides a check list for action if you want to stop or change a development to which you object.

THE SYSTEM

Planning decisions are usually taken by local government. The system is supervised by the Secretary of State for the Environment (or Wales or Scotland) who also lays down policies that local government must follow.

There are three tiers of local government in the countryside: parish council (or town council, in the case of small towns), district council and county council. In Scotland and Wales, the equivalent of the parish/town council is the community council. (The Scottish community councils, though statutorily elected, have no formal powers.) Parish councils do not decide planning applications, but they have considerable influence over the visual appearance of villages. Their powers include the provision and maintenance of clocks, footpaths, village halls, litterbins, some street lighting, car parks, ponds, lavatories, seats, shelters and signs. They can go out and buy street furniture, such as benches and bollards. The district councils will always seek their opinion on questions affecting their areas (though this is not to say that they will act on it). In the British system of government, the parish council is a rare example of local democracy. Make the most of it.

Elections generally take place on the same day as those for the district council. Unfortunately a turn out of as little as 25 per cent is considered 'extremely good', according to Paul Clayden of the National Association of Local Councils, and since there are often not enough candidates to fill the posts available, many councillors get in unopposed. Meetings are held in public, and three days' advance notice must be given by posting notices in prominent places. These will include the parish notice board, itself a pre-eminent piece of street furniture. Funding comes through the community charge, but the contribution of each parishioner is so small that charge capping is not an issue. Naturally the parish council's ability to safeguard the character of its area will depend on the energy and ability of its members – and of course their point of view. The danger of the parish council is that of all forms of local government: the people most prepared to take up the burdens of being a councillor are all too often those who stand to gain most from it by promoting development.

The parish council is often instrumental in drawing up the local plan for its area. The local plan should articulate the way in which local residents hope that their village or town will develop over the next ten or fifteen years. District councils are not obliged to adopt the views expressed in local plans as part of their official policy, but generally they are sympathetic. Recently the government decreed that, by the mid 1990s, every area of England should be covered by a local plan. Some villages already have one, but many up and down the country do not. As a result hundreds of local plans are at present being prepared. This gives the residents of villages a supreme chance to have their say in what the future of their area will be like. Most people will be able to find out the address of their parish council by asking in the local post office. If that fails, however, a complete list of all the parish councils in the country is held by the National Association of Local Councils, 108 Great Russell Street, London WC1; tel: 071 637 1865/071 636 4929.

The next tier up, the district council, is for many people the most important, because it decides the bulk of planning applications. Officially all decisions are taken by the planning committee, made up of selected councillors. Naturally the chairman of the planning committee is a figure of power. Uncontested planning applications are not discussed by the committee. The planning committee is advised by a staff of professionally trained planners, led by the chief planning officer. Usually the planners welcome contact with the public. They are happy to explain the applications that are lodged with them, and to indicate what course of action may be appropriate to objectors. Most district councils employ at least one conservation officer, with particular experience of historic buildings.

The district council is responsible for approving and publishing the local plan. Another important function of the district council is to declare conservation areas.

The county council establishes the broad strategy for the development of the whole county. This is embodied in a cardinally important document: the county structure plan. County structure plans balance the aspirations of the districts against, ideally, a wider view of the priorities for the county. They are the definitive, legally binding documents to which the local plans must conform. When in draft, they are subject to a long process of public consultation, and anyone concerned about the future of the county must certainly register his or her comments at this stage. Finally they must be agreed with the Secretary of State. He appoints a committee of experts to examine them and call witnesses. That process is known as the 'Examination in Public'. Once 'adopted' the county structure plans form the basis of planning policy for more than a decade. They will often be quoted in public inquiries. They cover many areas of interest: shops, factories, housing, towns and cities, transport, waste disposal, tourism, leisure facilities, green belts, agriculture, social services and so on. One subject that has lately caused heated debate is the number of new houses to be built within the period of the plan. This can cause friction between the county council and the D.o.E., or even between the county council and its districts.

The county council also decides planning applications for very large projects, major new settlements, new through roads and mineral extraction. Mineral extraction includes sand and gravel workings.

The addresses and telephone numbers of all district and county councils can be found in the *Directory of Official Architecture and Planning* (Longman, published annually); this also lists the names of the chief planning officers.

The National Parks are the exception to the rule. Each National Park has a single authority which takes all planning decisions, in consultation with the district and county councils. The councils nominate two thirds of the members of the National Park Authority, while the rest are appointed by the Secretary of State. (A criticism of the National Parks is that none of the members is directly responsible to an electorate.) The Authority produces a National Park Management Plan, equivalent to a county structure plan.

Overseeing the whole process is the Secretary of State. In England and Northern Ireland this will be the Secretary of State for the Environment; elsewhere the Secretary of State for Scotland or Wales. The Secretary of State establishes the ground rules by which local government must play. If he feels any issue is too big for the district council or county council to determine on their own, or if he believes that they would find it difficult to be impartial, he can 'call it in' for his personal decision. Applicants who feel that they have been unjustly refused planning permission can appeal to the Secretary of State. However, there is no right of appeal for third parties, including objectors. Call-ins and appeals generally involve a public inquiry. In this case an inspector is appointed by the Secretary of State to hear the evidence from everyone who is involved. Public inquiries are apt to be long winded affairs, in which the principal players have legal representation. Witnesses are cross-examined on their evidence, as in a court of law.

Over the last decade planning policy in England has been increasingly directed by the Department of the Environment. It is therefore all the more important that the Secretary of State should know your views on the countryside. The D.o.E.'s address is shown on page 130.

WHAT TO DO IN A CRISIS

Let us imagine that while walking through a village, you have seen a sheet of white paper, wrapped up in plastic, attached to a gatepost or telegraph pole. When you read it, you find it is notice of a planning application to alter an existing building or erect a new one. You do not like the sound of it. What should you do? These are the steps to follow if you want your voice to be heard.

– First you should go to the district council and ask to see the plans. They will usually be on show for a period of twenty-one days after being lodged. This is also the period within which objections must be received. Remember that some of these days may well have elapsed before you saw the notice: you will have to move quickly.

You may find that the district council publishes a guide on how to obtain or oppose planning permission, which you should obtain.

– Discuss the plans with the planning officer. He will explain whether he thinks that the developer could be persuaded to modify his scheme.

In a recent case in Norfolk (see page 50), a developer applied to build seven bungalows on a sensitive site near the entrance to the village. A local artist objected and sketched what he thought would be a much better development, in the form of a terrace. The planners indicated to the developer that, if something on these lines was submitted, it would receive planning permission. So the developer took it up and built it.

– If you decide to object, write to the district council. You cannot register objections by telephone. Nor, if you want your objection to be considered by the planning committee, is it possible to have it kept confidential. You might just remember that the usual laws of libel apply!

Keep your letter pithy, relevant and logical. (There is nothing to be gained by being abusive.) Say whether you think the scheme ugly or unsuitable to the location, but try to base your arguments on established planning policy for the area, as set out in the local plan or county structure plan. The development may not conform in terms of use (e.g. a noisy factory in what is meant to be a residential area); it may put undue strain on the roads and services (water supply, for example); it may spoil an amenity, such as an open space. The planning committee will base their decision on what they believe is in the best interest of the community as a whole.

Most people are best advised to write their own letters rather than using a lawyer. Planning committees tend to find the personal approach more convincing.

Correspondence should be addressed impersonally to the chief planning officer. It can be marked 'for the attention of Mr X' if you know who is handling the case, but the reply will invariably be signed by the chief planning officer. If you think that the planning staff have already been swayed by the developer, copy your letters to the chairman of the planning committee. Excellent advice on writing letters, with examples, is given in *The Which? Guide to Planning and Conservation* (details below).

– Make sure that the parish (or town) council and, if there is one, the local amenity society are on your side. Many amenity societies have considerable experience of planning matters and will be able to give practical help.

The Civic Trust (address on page 129) has a list of about one thousand amenity societies registered with it.

– If there is no amenity society, start one. The Civic Trust can supply a 'starter pack'. This will include a model constitution which will save the enormous labour of drawing one up from scratch.

One benefit of having a local amenity society is that the district council will generally keep it informed of planning applications as they come in. Otherwise, short of spotting the notices when they are posted, concerned village residents can find it difficult to discover what is being proposed until too late. Even neighbours and the parish council do not have the statutory right to be informed of all planning applications by letter. Major applications must be advertised in the press, so keep an eye on the small ads pages of the local newspaper.

– Lobby your own district councillor and everyone on the planning committee, starting with the chairman. Probably a face to face meeting will be the best way of doing this, but the choice of tactics must depend on the personalities involved.

– Raise a petition. Petitions tend to be looked upon with some scepticism by planning authorities, since Mickey Mouse signatures and the 'I'll-do-anything-to-make-him-go-away' factor ensure that signatures can be obtained for almost any cause. The most effective petitions are those which truly demonstrate a very strong measure of local support. Be sure that everyone who signs gives his or her address.

– Start a correspondence in the local paper or, if the issue is of sufficiently broad interest, in the national press.

An amenity society should think of issuing a press release. This should, if possible, take the form of a single sheet of headed paper, giving a punchy account of the case: the shorter the better. Put the most newsworthy fact in the first sentence. The press release should be sent to any named journalists who might be interested, and to the News Editor of the local paper, radio and television stations. It must end with the line: 'For further information please contact . . .', giving a name and telephone number.

– Enlist the support of any national body to whom the case is relevant (see Chapter 22).

– It may be sensible to write to the chairman of the organization perpetrating the deed. Perhaps he is not aware of what is happening, or of the environmental consequences, or the bad publicity that will ensue.

In the case of a red telephone box, contact your local British Telecom payphone manager. Payphone managers seem to be allowed more discretion in keeping boxes than official BT policy would suggest. Some payphone managers are more sympathetic to the cause than others.

– Consider writing to your Member of Parliament. If a developer from outside the area is stirring up a hornet's nest of local opposition, he may pursue the case. Naturally his support will be important where the developer is actually a government department. But he is unlikely to intervene in a dispute between two constituents. You must also face the possibility that he might side with what you regard as the opposition.

– If you feel that the case is sufficiently important or controversial to be called in by the Secretary of State for the Environment, you must make your request for him to do so before planning permission is given. It will be too late afterwards. The request will carry more weight if it can be shown that there is enormous public feeling on the issue.

Special planning constraints govern listed buildings and conservation areas. Buildings are listed because of their 'special architectural or historic interest'. If you do not know whether a building is listed or not, the district council will be able to tell you. There is a complete set of the lists covering England at the National Monuments Record, 23 Savile Row, London, W1X 1AB.

There are three categories of listed building: Grade 2, Grade 2* and Grade 1. Each grade indicates a different level of importance. Whatever the grade, listed building consent must be sought for any demolition or extension; this applies just as much to the inside as to the outside of the building. Listed building consent must also be sought for any alteration which would affect its special architectural or historical character (in some cases this could include painting).

The five statutorily recognized national amenity societies – the Ancient Monuments Society, the Society for the Protection of Ancient Buildings, the Georgian Group, the Victorian Society and the Council for British Archaeology – receive notice of planning applications affecting all the listed buildings in Britain.

There are 6,500 conservation areas in Britain. As I have shown (page 64), the legislation does little to protect individual buildings from alteration. It does, however, require that conservation area consent be obtained for demolitions. In theory no new building is permitted which does not enhance the character of the conservation area, but in practice this is not always the case.

Objections relating to listed buildings and conservation areas will be more persuasive if they show a grasp of the history and architecture involved. You may therefore wish to consult or even join the national amenity society responsible for the relevant period of building. The Ancient Monuments Society handles cases of all dates. The period reference for the others is generally as follows: Society for the Protection of Ancient Buildings, before 1700; Georgian Group, 1700–1837; Victorian Society, 1837–1914; Thirties Society, after 1914. In addition there are a number of societies specializing in particular building types – for example, the Cinema Theatre Association (to do with cinemas) and the Folly Fellowship (to do with follies).

To get a building listed, you can write to the Head of Listing, Department of the Environment, Room C9–10, 2 Marsham Street, London SW1P 3EB. They will consult with English Heritage. You will need to supply an architectural/historical description, photographs from as many angles as possible and an extract from the relevant Ordnance Survey map. In practice it is easier to make the application through the relevant national amenity society, which will be well used to it. That is assuming that the amenity society agrees with you that the building is indeed worthy of listing: it will not wish to compromise its own standing with the D.o.E. by submitting what it regards as a complete no-hoper.

All historic buildings legislation is contained in the D.o.E. circular 8/87, which is available from HMSO.

Further reading. Most people will find all the advice they need on the workings of the planning system in *The Which? Guide to Planning and Conservation*, written by John Willman (Consumers' Association and Hodder and Stoughton, 1990). If more detailed coverage is required, the following are some of the standard works, written for professionals:

Sir Desmond Heap (ed.), *Encyclopedia of Law and Practice Planning*, 4 vols, with quarterly updates (Sweet and Maxwell, 1959–present).
Charles Mynors, *Listed Buildings and Conservation Areas* (Longman, 1989).
Charles Mynors, *Planning Applications and Appeals* (Architectural Press, 1987).
Roger Suddards, *Listed Buildings Law and Practice* (Sweet and Maxwell, 2nd edn, 1988).

21

HEROES
AND ANTI-HEROES
OF THE COUNTRYSIDE

HEROES

The future of the countryside rests in the hands of individuals. To emphasize this point I would like to invest a number of individuals with a newly invented order, Hero of the British Countryside. As yet the decoration does not bring with it so much as a medal, but I believe that the people to whom it is offered more than deserve to have their achievements in defending the countryside, or enhancing its beauty and variety, recognized in some way.

The Lady ALDINGTON, founder of the Jacob's Sheep Society.

Carola BALLARD, for starting a local brewery, Ballards, in Petersfield, Hampshire.

Sir Derek BARBER, former chairman of the Countryside Commission and founder member of the Farming and Wildlife Advisory Group.

Leslie BARKER, Dorset veterinary surgeon, for exemplary care of animals.

Jennifer BEAZLEY, chairman of the National Association of Decorative and Fine Arts Society's Church Recorders, who are compiling a comprehensive inventory of the contents of parish churches throughout Britain.

Mr and Mrs John BERRY, for the 130 species of wildflower that have been counted on Billingsmoor Farm.

Sir Richard BODY, pioneer campaigner for less intensive agriculture, the use of fewer chemicals and the treatment of animals with respect.

Will BURDETT, retired farmer, for the keeping of Orpington and Buff Orpington chickens.

Christopher BURNETT, landscape consultant to the Eaton and Holkham estates in Cheshire and Norfolk.

Douglas CAMPBELL, blacksmith to the National Trust for Scotland, for repairing gates, statues, fountains and lanterns throughout Scotland.

Steven CHANT, secretary of the Master Thatchers' Association.

Harry CLEGG of Humberts, a land agent who has secured the future of many country estates.

Sue CLIFFORD, co-founder of Common Ground, for furthering, through the arts, conservation and publishing, greater understanding and love of the countryside.

Peter CLOSE, of Berwick-on-Tweed and Phil EVANS, of Ross-on-Wye, for keeping herds of Longhorn cattle.

Benjamin COOKE, for services to horse riding, Burnham, Buckinghamshire.

J. R. COWARD, chairman of the Sutton Hastoe Housing Association, for low cost village housing, admirably designed.

Nicholas CRAWLEY, the imagination behind Historic House Hotels Ltd, owners of Bodysgallen Hall, Middlethorpe Hall and Hartwell Hall.

The Lord CRICKHOWELL, chairman of the National Rivers Authority, for an unexpected display of teeth.

Duff Hart DAVIS, for his Saturday column in *The Independent*.

Susan DENYER, mastermind of the National Trust's vernacular buildings and landscape surveys.

The Duchess of DEVONSHIRE, the power behind a great country estate employing 170 people.

Mrs Maldwin DRUMMOND, founding chairman of the Hampshire Gardens Trust: thanks to the efforts of the Trust, many previously neglected historic gardens in the county have been revived.

The Lord DULVERTON, for the Batsford Arboretum, Gloucestershire.

Susie and Ivor DUNKERTON, for traditional cider-making at Pembridge, Herefordshire.

Alastair J. DYMOND, development director of the Rare Breeds Survival Trust, for helping preserve Norfolk Horn sheep.

Her Majesty Queen ELIZABETH the Queen Mother, farmer in Caithness.

Sebastian de FERRANTI, for building a rotunda in Cheshire.

The Lord FEVERSHAM, for moving back into Duncombe Park, formerly a girls' school, and honouring it with the wittiest guidebook in England.

Ian Hamilton FINLAY, artist, poet and the reviver of the philosophical garden.

David FLEMING, chairman of the Soil Association, for attempting to unravel the woolly thinking of the green movement.

R. A. FORD, Joint Master of the Quantock Hunt, for helping to ensure that there are still deer on Exmoor.

Reverend Ronald FROST, vicar of Kimbolton, for making a success of the vicarage, which had mushrooms growing on the drawing room floor when he arrived.

John Paul GETTY II, for rescuing the fields at Ely Cathedral from the clutches of the rural dean, and resuscitating the Wormsley estate.

Princess Alice, Duchess of GLOUCESTER, for annual attendance at the Peterborough Hound Show.

Sir James GOLDSMITH, financier, for turning green.

Terry GOLDSMITH, for thirty years spent arguing against the kind of reckless economic growth that destroys the countryside.

Sir Simon GOURLAY, former president of the National Farmers Union, for accepting that the farm support structure must enhance the countryside.

Jenny GREENE, editor of *Country Life*, for upholding the standards of civilized life in the countryside.

The Lord GRIMOND, for services to Orkney.

The GOVERNOR, HM Young Offenders Institution, Hollesley Bay, Suffolk, for his splendid teams of Suffolk horses.

Johnny GRANT, for revitalizing the Highland estate of Rothiemurchis.

Joanna HANNAM, of the Norfolk Society, for her energy in stirring up constructive protest to unsympathetic development in East Anglia.

Wilhemina, Lady HARROD, founder-president of the Norfolk Churches Trust, for helping to preserve many of the over 600 churches that are an essential part of Norfolk's mysterious, if rather flat, landscape.

Joe HENSON, founder chairman of the Rare Breeds Survival Trust and a champion of Castlemilk Moorit sheep.

Patrick HERON, artist, for campaigning to protect the beauty of his native Cornwall.

Michael HESELTINE, for reviving the nabob spirit at Thenford.

Patrick HOLDEN, director of British Organic Farmers, for twenty years' commitment to the organic farming movement, put into practice on his farm in Wales.

Professor William George HOSKINS, for telling us that the British countryside was formed by man in books such as *The Making of the English Landscape*.

The parish council of HOUGHTON AND WYTON, in Cambridgeshire, for having the imagination to install new, locally made street lights to a sympathetic design, rather than the usual sodium horrors.

Gervase JACKSON-STOPS, architectural adviser to the National Trust and organizer of the Washington Treasure Houses exhibition, for ubiquity.

Professor Peter JEWELL, of the Research Group in Mammalian Ecology and Reproduction, Cambridge, for keeping Soay sheep.

Francis JOHNSON, for a lifetime spent enhancing and repairing the architecture of Yorkshire.

J. Raymond JOHNSTONE, chairman of the Forestry Commission, for repenting of the mistakes of his predecessors.

Sir William KESWICK, whose patronage encouraged Henry Moore, and therefore the rest of the world, to place sculpture in the open air.

Angela KING, co-founder of Common Ground. *See* Sue Clifford.

Paddy KITCHEN, clerk to Barnswell Parish Council.

Sibylle KREUTZBERGER and Pam SCHWERDT, for gardening at Sissinghurst, Kent.

Leon KRIER, for arguing for the better planning of cities which would relieve pressure on the countryside.

Stephen LAMBERT, vicar of St Mary's, Chastleton, for his past mastership of the Heythrop Hunt.

David LEA, architect and small-holder, for the design of low-energy buildings.

David LEARMONT, master historian of the country house kitchen.

Richard LOMBE-TAYLOR, for replanting 37 miles of hedgerow on his Norfolk estate.

The Duke of MARLBOROUGH, for replanting the Blenheim landscape so that it may survive into the 24th century.

Kit MARTIN, for showing that derelict country houses need not be demolished but, like his own many triumphs, can be converted to appropriate new uses – even continuing as family houses.

Stephen MATTICK, architect, for showing that speculative houses do not have to be eyesores.

The Lord MELCHETT, former president of the Ramblers' Association and now executive director of Greenpeace, who created inalienable rights of way as part of a new system of footpaths across his Norfolk farm.

Ian NIALL, writer, for opening the eyes of townspeople to the realities of the countryside.

Graham OVENDEN, painter, musician, photographer, collector, ruralist and the builder of his own home, Barley Splatt.

Anthony du Gard PASLEY, a designer who understands how gardens should be integrated into the countryside.

Peter PALUMBO, for turning his whole Berkshire estate over to organic farming.

George PLUMTRE, for his support of village cricket.

John PIPER, the genius of place.

Jonathon PORRITT, campaigner extraordinary for man's gentler treatment of Nature.

The PRINCE OF WALES, for saving the National Apple Collection at Brogdale in Kent.

Jeremy PURSEGLOVE, for bringing Nature back into water management.

Jack QUINE, farmer, for helping to save the Manx Loghtan sheep.

Major Patrick RANCE, the maestro of cheese, whose specialist shop in Streatley, Berkshire, showed that not all need be gloom and doom in the village store.

The Duke of RICHMOND and Gordon, for replanting the Goodwood estate after 250,000 trees were blown down in the Great Storm of 1987.

David SHORT, publican of the Queen's Head, Newton, for the best roast beef sandwiches in England.

John SIMPSON, architect, for reinventing the art of planning villages.

Colin Stansfield SMITH, Hampshire's County Architect, for bringing good architecture into the countryside.

Sir John SMITH, founder of the Landmark Trust and saviour of two hundred delightful buildings.

Freddie STOCKDALE, founder of Pavilion Opera, for enhancing the store of entertainment in country houses.

Sir James STORMONTH DARLING, former Director of the National Trust for Scotland, for saving mountains for the nation.

George STYLES, farmer, for befriending the Gloucester Old Spot pig.

The Lady TANKERVILLE, of Chillingham Castle, Northumberland, for preserving the ancient breed of Chillingham cattle.

Franco TARUSCHIO, of the Walnut Tree restaurant, for bringing white truffles to Abergavenny.

Quinlan TERRY, for decades of work in Dedham, showing that it is possible to extend an old village without spoiling it.

Bernard TIDMARSH, third generation farrier in Gloucestershire, for keeping innumerable horses on their feet.

Rosemary VEREY, for one of the most beautiful of all modern gardens, in Barnsley, Gloucestershire.

Simon VERITY, stone carver, for breathing fresh life into the art of the funerary monument.

The Lord VINSON, for revitalizing the Rural Development Commission.

Martin WALTON, landscape painter and chairman of the Ludham Society, Norfolk, for persuading local developers to redesign new housing developments in keeping with the Norfolk vernacular.

J. N. P. WATSON, the doyen of hunting writers, for advocacy of animal welfare.

Wilfrid WELD, for commissioning and publishing a model survey of the landscape history of the Weld estate in Dorset.

The Earl of WEMYSS AND MARCH, for championing the plants and animals of the Scottish countryside.

Thomas WHEATLEY-HUBBARD, farmer, for supporting the cause of Tamworth pigs.

David WHEELER, proprietor and publisher of the erudite and elegant gardening magazine *Hortus*.

Sir William WILKINSON, merchant banker, chairman of the Nature Conservancy Council, who made the NCC believe in itself.

Adrian WOODHOUSE, writer, for antiquarianism at Snitterton Hall.

Lawrence WOODWARD, director of Elm Farm Research Centre, the only research organization to specialize in organic agriculture.

Barry WOOKEY, for his model organic farm at Rushall, in Wiltshire.

Sir Marcus WORSLEY, for forestry at Hovingham in Yorkshire, carried out with the aid of a working horse.

Richard and Rosamund YOUNG, for producing highly sought-after organic meat on Kites Nest Farm near Broadway.

ANTI-HEROES

Even as I write, a team of several dozen hand-picked researchers is busily at work preparing a roll of all those anti-heroes of the country-side whom the rest of us may wish immediately to strike off our dinner party lists. But perhaps this is not the place to publish it in full. After all, my aim in writing this book has been to take a positive line, and I have tried not so much to dwell on the disasters of the past as to show what can be done to improve the future.

What I can offer is a foretaste of the jam that the completed roll (a Swiss one) will contain. Entries are organized under the categories below. No doubt many readers will already possess personal registers of offenders, based on their own local observations of the countryside. You may like to insert supplementary names in the margins of this book, which are wide enough to allow ample annotation.

Each category is followed by an example, but don't imagine that he or she is necessarily the only one that could be included. There are many, many others.

Farmers who talk of turning Cambridgeshire into Kansas (and other counties into places equally unattractive):
Oliver WALSTON, farmer and agricultural journalist.

Companies who have been slow to catch the new mood of environmental concern:
J. F. KERRIDGE, chairman of Fisons, for peat digging.

Organizations that turn a blind eye to the damage that unrestrained tourism is doing in the countryside:
William DAVIS, chairman of the British Tourist Authority (he considers 'Tourism is one of Britain's great success stories').

Recently privatized companies who throw over solid tradition and an image of public service in their search for a zappy new corporate look:
Iain VALLANCE, chairman of British Telecom and Lord High Executioner of the red telephone box.

Politicians who have sought to minimize the aesthetic control that planners can operate over new development:

Michael HESELTINE, Secretary of State for the Environment when the planning system was overhauled in 1980.

Intensive poultry and livestock farmers whose operations detract from their surroundings:
Bernard 'Bootiful' MATTHEWS, the Norfolk turkey farmer.

Idealists who misguidedly believe that if the British countryside returned to wilderness it would still be beautiful:
Rodney LEGGE, chairman of the Open Spaces Society.

Councillors who permit unsympathetic development in historic towns:
Councillor John KNIGHT, leader of the St Edmundsbury Borough Council, for allowing the present scheme for the Cattle Market site in Bury St Edmunds.

Hoteliers who deposit strings of gaudy eating places along trunk roads:
The Lord FORTE, chairman of Trusthouse Forte Plc, owners of both the Little Chef and Happy Eater chains.

Anyone who could improve the poverty of design in new housing estates, but doesn't:
Sir Eric POUNTAIN, chairman of Tarmac Plc.

Those responsible for allowing new vicarages to take the form of ranch-style bungalows:
Sir Douglas LOVELOCK, First Church Estates Commissioner.

Successive Secretaries of State who have made the Department of Transport into the Department of the Motor car:
The Rt Honourable Paul CHANNON, the Rt Honourable Cecil PARKINSON, the Rt Honourable Malcolm RIFKIND etc. etc.

Builders of marinas and related housing developments around the coast:
Peter de SAVARY, for his scheme at Hayle in Cornwall.

Do-it-yourself stores that purvey unsightly doors and windows:
Geoff POWELL, chairman of B&Q.

Grocery retailers who build new superstores by the dozen:
The Lord SAINSBURY of Preston Candover, chairman of J. Sainsbury Plc.

The big breweries who close down little ones:
Alick RANKIN, chairman of Scottish and Newcastle Breweries (they also own Center Parcs).

Landowners who have converted old barns into houses:
The Prince of WALES, who has done this at Caradon in the Duchy of Cornwall.

Engineers who favour the triumph of technology over wildlife and landscape:
John BAKER, chief executive of National Power Plc, prominent in the campaign to build the Sizewell B nuclear power station.

Grandees who have given up their country houses and retired beyond these shores:
The Lord BROWNLOW, formerly of Belton House.

Publishers who sell guidebooks that direct more and more people towards already over-visited parts of the landscape, without taking precautions to ensure that their impact is minimized:
The past and present executives of MICHAEL JOSEPH Ltd. They are responsible for the excellent series of guides to walking in the Lake District and elsewhere, written by the late Alfred Wainwright. Unfortunately, while Wainwright himself deplored visitors wearing out paths, his books were one of the chief reasons why they were on them in the first place.

Clearing banks who mercilessly apply their logos across the facades of old buildings:
Sir John QUINTON, chairman of Barclays Bank.

People who build Burger King-style houses in the green belt:
The Duke and Duchess of YORK, owners of the OK Yah Corral in Windsor Great Park.

22

HEAVENLY BODIES: WHO TO GO TO FOR ADVICE AND INFORMATION

Action with Communities in Rural
England (ACRE),
Stroud Road, Cirencester,
Gloucestershire GL7 6JR;
tel: 0285 653477

Agricultural Development and
Advisory Service (ADAS),
First Floor, Nobel House,
17 Smith Square,
London SW1P 3JR;
tel: 071 238 5619/5632

Ancient Monuments Society,
St Andrews by the Wardrobe,
Queen Victoria Street,
London EC4V 5DE;
tel: 071 236 3934; 071 489 8695

Architectural Heritage Fund,
17 Carlton House Terrace,
London SW1 5AW;
tel: 071 925 0199

Arkleton Trust
Enstone,
Oxfordshire OX7 4HH;
tel: 0608 677 255
Studies new approaches to rural
education and development in Europe
and the Third World.

British Association for Shooting and
Conservation (BASC),
Marford Mill,
Rossett, Wrexham,
Clwyd LL12 0HL;
tel: 0244 570 881

British Field Sports Society (BFSS),
59 Kennington Road,
London SE1 7PZ;
tel: 071 928 4742

British Trust for Conservation
Volunteers,
36 St Mary's Street,
Wallingford,
Oxfordshire OX10 0EU;
tel: 0491 39766

British Trust for Ornithology,
Beech Grove,
Tring,
Hertfordshire HP3 5NR;
tel: 044282 3461

Church Commissioners,
1 Millbank,
Westminster,
London SW1P 3JZ;
tel: 071 222 7010
Responsible for the management of
the greater part of the Church of
England's historic assets, including
over 150,000 acres of agricultural
land.

Civic Trust,
17 Carlton House Terrace,
London SW1Y 5AW;
tel: 071 930 0914
Campaigns on behalf of the built
environment. The annual Civic Trust
Awards aim to raise design standards
of new buildings.

Common Ground,
London Ecology Centre,
45 Shelton Street,
London WC2H 9HJ;
tel: 071 379 3109
Works to encourage new ways of
looking at our local environment
through all branches of the arts.

Conservation Trust,
George Palmer School,
Northumberland Avenue,
Reading,
Berkshire RG2 0EN;
tel: 0734 868 442
Runs a public enquiry service on
environmental topics and provides
consultancy and research services in
the field of conservation.

Council for the Care of Churches,
83 London Wall,
London EC2M 5NA;
tel: 071 638 0971

Council for Environmental
Education,
School of Education,
University of Reading,
London Road,
Reading,
Berkshire RG1 5AQ;
tel: 0734 875 123

Council for National Parks,
London Ecology Centre,
45 Shelton Street,
London WC2H 9HJ;
tel: 071 240 3603

Council for the Protection of Rural
England,
25 Buckingham Palace Road,
London SW1W 0PP;
tel: 071 976 6433

Council for the Protection of Rural
Wales,
Ty Gwyn,
31 High Street,
Welshpool,
Powys SY21 7JP;
tel: 0938 552 525

Country Landowners Association,
16 Belgrave Square,
London SW1X 8PQ;
tel: 071 235 0511
Agricultural lobbying body
representing landowners at local,
national and European government
levels.

The Countryside Commission,
John Dower House,
Crescent Place,
Cheltenham,
Gloucestershire GL50 3RA;
tel: 0242 521381
The leading organization concerned
with landscape conservation and
informal recreation in the
countryside in England and Wales.
Designates national parks and areas
of outstanding natural beauty.

Department of Agriculture and
Fisheries for Scotland,
Pentland House,
47 Robbs Loan,
Edinburgh EH14 1TW;
tel: 031 556 8400

Department of Agriculture for
Northern Ireland,
Dundonald House,
Upper Newtownards Road,
Belfast BT4 3SB;
tel: 0232 650 111

Department of the Environment,
2 Marsham Street,
London SW1P 3EB;
tel: 071 276 0554

Department of Transport,
2 Marsham Street,
London SW1P 3EB;
tel: 071 276 0800

English Heritage (Historic Buildings
and Monuments Commission for
England),
Fortress House,
23 Savile Row,
London W1X 1AB;
tel: 071 973 3000

The Environment Council,
80 York Way,
London N1 9AG;
tel: 071 278 4736
The umbrella body for UK
organizations concerned with the
environment.

The Farm and Rural Buildings
Centre,
National Agricultural Centre,
Stoneleigh,
Kenilworth,
Warwickshire CV8 2LG;
tel: 0203 696503

Farming and Wildlife Trust,
National Agricultural Centre,
Stoneleigh,
Kenilworth,
Warwickshire CV8 2RX;
tel: 0203 696699

Forestry Commission,
231 Corstorphine Road,
Edinburgh EH12 7AT;
tel: 031 334 0303

Friends of the Earth,
26–28 Underwood Street,
London N1 7JQ;
tel: 071 490 1555

The Game Conservancy Trust,
Burgate Manor,
Fordingbridge,
Hampshire SP6 1EF;
tel: 0425 652381
Undertakes research into game and
game habitats.

The Georgian Group,
37 Spital Square,
London E1 6DY;
tel: 071 377 1722
Campaigns for the protection and
enjoyment of Georgian buildings,
monuments, parks and gardens.

Green Party,
10 Station Parade,
Balham High Road,
London SW12 9AZ;
tel: 071 673 0045

The Hawk Trust,
c/o Birds of Prey Section,
Zoological Society of London,
Regent's Park,
London NW1 4RY;
tel: 071 722 3333

Her Majesty's Inspectorate of
Pollution,
see Department of the Environment

Heritage Coast Forum,
Centre for Environmental
Interpretation,
Manchester Polytechnic,
St Augustines,
Lower Chaltham Street,
Manchester M15 6BY;
tel: 061 247 2000 ext. 1073

Historic Buildings and Monuments
Directorate (Scotland),
20 Brandon Street,
Edinburgh EH3 5RA;
tel: 031 556 8400

Historic Churches Preservation
Trust,
Fulham Palace,
London SW6 6EA;
tel: 071 736 3054

Historic Houses Association,
38 Ebury Street,
London SW1W 0LU;
tel: 071 730 9419

Housing Corporation,
149 Tottenham Court Road,
London W1P 0BN;
tel: 071 387 9466
Lends government money to, and
supervises activities of, housing
associations.

The Landmark Trust,
21 Dean's Yard,
London SW1P 3PA;
tel: 071 222 6581
Charity which restores and
maintains distressed historic
buildings and lets them out for
holidays.

Landscape Institute,
12 Carlton House Terrace,
London SW1Y 5AH;
tel: 071 738 9166
Accrediting body for courses in
landscape architecture and
management. Aims to promote the
highest standard of service in these
professions.

Men of the Trees,
Sandy Lane,
Crawley Down,
West Sussex RH10 4HS;
tel: 0342 712 536
Encourages the planting and
protection of trees and woodland
throughout the UK.

Ministry of Agriculture, Fisheries
and Food (MAFF),
Whitehall Place,
London SW1A 2HH;
tel: 071 270 3000

National Agricultural Centre Rural
Trust,
35 Belgrave Square,
London SW1X 8QN;
tel: 071 245 6998

National Farmers' Union (NFU),
Agriculture House,
Knightsbridge,
London SW1X 7NJ;
tel: 071 225 5077

National Gardens Scheme Charitable
Trust,
Hatchlands Park,
East Clandon,
Guildford,
Surrey GU4 7RT;
tel: 0483 211 535
Raises funds for a range of charities
through the opening of private
gardens on certain days during the
year.

National Heritage Memorial Fund
(NHMF),
10 St James's Street,
London SW1A 1EF;
tel: 071 930 0963

National Parks Commission,
see Countryside Commission

National Rivers Authority (NRA),
30–34 Albert Embankment,
London SE1 7TL;
tel: 071 820 0101

National Rural Enterprise Centre
(NREC),
National Agricultural Centre,
Royal Agricultural Society of
England,
Stoneleigh, Warwickshire CV8 2LZ;
tel: 0203 696969

The National Trust,
36 Queen Anne's Gate,
London SW1H 9AS;
tel: 071 222 9251

The National Trust for Scotland,
5 Charlotte Square,
Edinburgh EH2 4DU;
tel: 031 226 5922

Natural Environment Research
Council (NERC),
Polaris House,
North Star Avenue,
Swindon,
Wiltshire SN2 1EU;
tel: 0793 411623

The Nature Conservancy Council,
Northminster House,
Northminster Road,
Peterborough,
Cambridgeshire PE1 1UA;
tel: 0733 340345

Open Spaces Society,
25a Bell Street,
Henley-on-Thames,
Oxfordshire RG9 2BA;
tel: 0491 573 535
Works to free all areas of common
ground for legal public access.
Britain's oldest national conservation
body.

Peak and Northern Footpaths
Society,
15 Parkfield Drive,
Tyldesley,
Manchester M29 8NR;
tel: 061 790 4383

Population Concern,
231 Tottenham Court Road,
London W1P 0HY;
tel: 071 637 9582

The Poultry Club of Great Britain,
Home Farm House,
Stratfield Saye,
Reading,
Berkshire RG7 2BT;
tel: 0256 880 253

Railway Heritage Trust,
Melton House,
65 Clarendon Road,
Watford,
Hertfordshire WD1 1DP;
tel: 0923 240250

The Ramblers' Association,
1–5 Wandsworth Road,
London SW8 2LJ;
tel: 071 582 6878/6826

Rare Breeds Survival Trust,
National Agricultural Centre,
Stoneleigh,
Kenilworth,
Warwickshire CV8 2BR;
tel: 0203 696551

The Redundant Churches Fund,
St Andrews by the Wardrobe,
Queen Victoria Street,
London EC4V 5DE;
tel: 071 248 7461

Royal Agricultural Society of England
(RASE),
National Agricultural Centre,
Stoneleigh,
Kenilworth,
Warwickshire CV8 2RX;
tel: 0203 696969 ext. 218

Royal Commission on the Historical
Monuments of England (RCHME),
Fortress House,
23 Savile Row,
London W1X 2JQ;
tel: 071 973 3351

Royal Forestry Society of England,
Wales and Northern Ireland,
102 High Street,
Tring,
Hertfordshire HP23 4AF;
tel: 044 282 2028

Royal Horticultural Society (RHS),
PO Box 313,
80 Vincent Square,
London SW1P 2PE;
tel: 071 834 4333

Royal Institute of British Architects
(RIBA),
66 Portland Place,
London W1N 4AD;
tel: 071 580 5533

Royal Society for Nature
Conservation,
The Green,
Nettleham,
Lincoln LN2 2NR;
tel: 0522 544 400

Royal Society for the Protection of
Birds,
The Lodge,
Sandy,
Bedfordshire SG19 2NR;
tel: 0767 80551

The Rural Development Commission,
11 Cowley Street,
London SW1;
tel: 071 276 6969

The Sand and Gravel Association Ltd,
1 Bramber Court,
2 Bramber Road,
London W14 9PB;
tel: 071 381 8778
Represents 90 of the UK's largest
sand and gravel producers. Runs an
award scheme to promote the
restoration of sites beyond statutory
obligations.

Sane Planning in the South East,
Polbathic,
Farley Hill,
Reading,
Berkshire RG7 1XE;
tel: 0734 760439

Save Britain's Heritage,
68 Battersea High Street,
London SW11 3HX;
tel: 071 228 3336

Scottish Conservation Projects Trust,
Balallan House,
24 Allan Park,
Stirling FK9 2QG;
tel: 0786 79697

Scottish Landowners Federation,
25 Maritime Street,
Edinburgh EH6 5PW;
tel: 031 555 1031

The Scottish Wildlife Trust,
25 Johnston Terrace,
Edinburgh EH1 2NH;
tel: 031 226 4602

Society for the Protection of Ancient
Buildings (SPAB),
37 Spital Square,
London E1 6DY;
tel: 071 377 1644

Society for the Responsible Use of
Resources in Agriculture and on the
Land (RURAL),
Home Close,
High Street,
Stonesfield,
Oxfordshire OX7 2PU;
tel: 0993 891 686

Soil Association,
86 Colston Street,
Bristol BS1 5BB;
tel: 0272 290 661
Sets standards for organic food
producers and campaigns for the
promotion of sustainable farming
methods.

The Thirties Society,
c/o Nicholas Long,
58 Crescent Lane,
London SW4;
tel: 071 622 7420

Timber Growers UK,
Admel House,
24 High Street,
Wimbledon Village,
London SW19 5DX;
tel: 081 944 6340

The Town and Country Planning
Association,
17 Carlton House Terrace,
London SW1Y 5AS;
tel: 071 930 8903

Transport 2000,
Walkden House,
10 Melton Street,
London NW1 3EJ;
tel: 071 388 8386
Campaigns for a sustainable national
transport policy which does least
damage to the environment.

Tree Council,
35 Belgrave Square,
London SW1X 8QN;
tel: 071 235 8854

The Victorian Society,
1 Priory Gardens,
London W4;
tel: 081 994 1019

The Woodland Trust,
Autumn Park,
Dysart Road,
Grantham,
Lincolnshire NG31 6LL;
tel: 0476 74297

World Pheasant Association (WPA),
PO Box 5,
Child Beale Wildlife Trust,
Lower Basildon,
Reading,
Berkshire RG8 9PF;
tel: 0734 845140